YESTERDAY'S CHILD

Christina J. Morrison

Islands Book Trust

Urras Leabhraichean nan Eilean
LIVING HISTORY

Published in 2016 by the Islands Book Trust

www.theislandsbooktrust.com

ISBN: 978-1-907443-68-8

The publisher would like to thank Donnie Morrison for the scanning and restoration of photographs and artefacts.

Islands Book Trust
Laxay Hall
Laxay
Isle of Lewis
HS2 9PJ
Tel: 01851 830316

Typeset by Erica Schwarz (www.schwarz-editorial.co.uk)
Cover design by Raspberry Creative Type, Edinburgh
Printed and bound by Martins the Printers, Berwick upon Tweed

Contents

About the Author

CHRISTINA JESSIE CHISHOLM MORRISON returned to Inverness after spending almost 50 years of her life on the Isle of Skye with her late husband Don where she brought up her family of five and worked in the community, serving as Registrar for North Skye. She and Don also enjoyed a few years' retirement in Gravir, Isle of Lewis, her parents' home village. Christina had many fond memories of growing up in her home town Inverness in the 1920s and '30s, some of which she relates in this book. Sadly Christina passed away on 10 January 2016, five weeks short of her 97th birthday and the publication date of this book. She was very much looking forward to seeing her book published.

Christina was brought up in Innes Street, Inverness, the middle child in a family of ten. The Chisholms were a musical family, her brothers were pipers, Christina and her sisters were dancers and her father Malcolm Chisholm was Pipe Major of the Royal British Legion Inverness. Theirs was a happy and lively household. Her father had seen action as a Seaforth Highlander in the South African campaigns, later joining the Queens' Own Cameron Highlanders. Some of her siblings were born at the Cameron Barracks in Inverness and her brothers later served with the Camerons during World War II.

Christina began her working life at the Town Clerk's office in Inverness (now the Town House). She assisted in the very early days of Highland tourism and, with keen sporting interests, worked for the National Fitness Council in the nascent Outward Bound Movement led by its famous founder Kurt Hahn. Christina joined the Auxiliary Territorial Service (ATS), the women's branch of the British Army set up in 1938. Once war was declared, Christina was instructed to go to London where she discovered that she would be working for

Military Intelligence at Whitehall, decoding top secret messages for Churchill's government. Christina's memory of the details of some of this work is extraordinary. Many of the messages she decoded related to events which, in hindsight, proved to be of great historical significance.

Read about Christina's adventures in wartime London and meeting Mr Churchill in his pyjamas! Christina's story is one of a life lived to the full and retold with modesty and humour.

PART I

GROWING UP IN INVERNESS

CHAPTER 1

'I Remember, I Remember'

(Thomas Hood)

U NLIKE the poet, I don't remember the house in Roseberry Place, Inverness where I was born, probably because I left it as a babe in arms and had it pointed out to me many years later when I had grown up. However what I do remember very clearly is the house in Innes Street, Inverness where I stayed until we moved to a modern house in another part of the town around the outbreak of World War II.

Some people can go back to shortly after their date of birth in their reminiscences but the farthest back I can remember is when I was about four, being brought round by my elder sister to the top of my mother's bed to peer through the brass railings and look at the lovely new baby my mother had in her arms. This was rather a special event because the baby was a little girl – only the third girl in a family of seven boys. I was the middle girl and the middle of the family, by age group, and I think I carried my 'middle' place all through my life, just being an average sort of person with average tastes in most areas.

The cosiest room in our house was the kitchen. This was a kitchen-cum-living-room where the cooking, dining and general day-to-day living was done. Adjacent to this was what we called, 'The Room' (no fancy names like 'sitting-room' or 'lounge' for us), where the piano stood and where we entertained special visitors and where we brought our friends when we were teenagers; but the hub of our universe was the kitchen, where my mother presided over us and, more often than not, a few of our neighbours' children. It was a large room with a high ceiling with skilfully fashioned cornices and to me it was the cosiest place on earth. There was a large kitchen range which formed a kind of ingle-nook, where we all gathered, sitting on chairs, stools or on the steel fender which was decorated with the words, 'Home Sweet Home' and which I sometimes liked to polish with a square of what we called emery cloth.

Every evening, when we were going to bed, my father placed our shoes in a row on the fender, "where the brownies will find them and polish them for the morning", he said. It was ages before I realised that HE was the brownie!

I often wonder where that fender went, as I remember it being replaced by a more modern one which had just a small kerb on it with two square box seats at each end and opened up like an ottoman and where books and magazines could be stored. My early memories were that we had oil or paraffin lamps for lighting but I remember having a gas cooker near the window where my mother did most of the cooking. We had progressed from gas to electricity by the time I had started school.

Modern houses seem to be full of draughts even with central heating but I don't remember ever feeling cold in our house. Perhaps this was because it always seemed to be full of people. I don't remember ever hearing anyone saying, "I'm bored and have nothing to do".

The day was too short for us and when darkness fell we made our own entertainment, playing board games or improvising indoor games. My father taught us to play draughts, chess and cards, although not for money. We played whist, rummy, 'beg o' my neighbour' (which we called 'please and thank you'), donkey pairs, sevens etc. All the while my mother would be knitting or sewing – and what patience she had! It wasn't unusual for her to sit at the table in the middle of the kitchen at her sewing machine while four of her seven sons marched around playing the bagpipes, sometimes two playing the melody and the other two playing the alto of such tunes as The Green Hills of Tyrol or Lord Lovat's Lament. This used to annoy me and I'd say, "I can't stand this awful racket" and I'd go off to 'The Room' to listen to Henry Hall or Jack Payne's Dance Band on the radio (which we called 'the wireless'); or I'd bang away at the piano to try to drown out the wails of the bagpipes. Today I'd love to hear the sound of their playing but, alas, all my brothers are now gone.

I think we were all quite well behaved children, as we were taught to respect our elders and never to interrupt their conversation unnecessarily. Good manners were appreciated in the home, the school and the street and we were usually careful that we didn't let the side down by not stepping off the pavement when an old lady came in the opposite direction and the boys often gave up their seats to ladies in the bus or train. Of course, 'boys will be boys' and there were times when the brothers couldn't resist in indulging in a bit of mischief but, if it went too far, they would hear about it when they got home. We girls weren't in the habit of 'clyping' (Invernessian for telling tales) but somehow or other our parents got wind of any unseemly conduct.

My mother disciplined the girls and my father attended to the boys but I never saw a belt in use. My mother had been a school monitor at one time and had in her possession a school strap, as we called it, southern Scots called it a 'tawse'. We had to hold out our hand, palm uppermost to get a flick with the strap for a misdemeanour, just as we would have received at school.

My father always wore a broad leather belt with two or three buckle fastenings around his waist and he called it his 'Cholera Belt'. No doubt it was a relic of his Army service in the East and it probably had held up his Cameron tartan kilt at one time. Although once or twice, I saw him unbuckling his belt threateningly when annoyed with one of his sons, the only thing I saw him using for striking them was his slipper. Oh boy, could he swipe with this slipper! It was mostly in evidence when he was teaching his sons to play the bagpipes. He taught them to read music and also taught them the finer parts of *Piobaireachd* (the classical music of the pipes) via the oral method called *Canntaireachd*. I remember hearing him shouting at them, "It isn't *Bo-para-ha* – it's *Bo-heelichum*!" Some of the brothers took to piping quite naturally but others had more difficulty and I used to feel sorry for them and felt glad that, although Daddy taught some girls (unwillingly) in his classes, he didn't want his daughters to learn.

Although girl pipers were taboo as far as Daddy was concerned, girl Highland dancers were approved by him and he taught several of them. As a Pipe-Major in the Cameron Highlanders, part of his job had been to teach Highland dancing to the pipers and officers. He had won many prizes for piping and dancing and used to judge at some of the Highland Games in the Highlands and Islands. He taught his eldest son Angus to dance and he in turn taught the younger members. My elder sister Marion taught me to dance the Highland Fling and most of the other dances but my brothers taught me my favourite dance, the Ghillie Callum sword dance. In my young days girl dancers were not allowed at some of the more prestigious Highland Games, for instance the Northern Meeting Games, the Cowal Gathering or the Nairn Games. Now the position is reversed and we rarely see male Highland dancers competing at the Games.

My favourite dancers of those days were R MacNiven Cuthbertson from the Glasgow area and James L MacKenzie of Aberdeen. It was a great triumph for my second eldest brother Kenneth when he beat Cuthbertson (the then World Champion Highland dancer) at the Nairn Games. There was a lady dancer called Mary Aitken from down Aberdeen/Banff way and I remember a family called Jessiman from Huntly who were all good dancers. I still see the name Jessiman in the prize lists of the Highland Games, so they must have passed on their skills to their descendants. Mary Aitken was a joy to watch, even until she was in her twenties as I remember. Bobby Watson was another Aberdeen dancer whom we admired but he and some other Aberdonian dancers thumped the back foot on the boards when doing the *pas-de-bas* and I called it the 'Aberdeen beat' because it seemed to be a localised habit. However, I noticed that my granddaughter Mairi used this 'beat' when she was being taught Highland dancing in Skye, so that is what her teacher obviously wanted. Times have changed in the Highland dancing scene with the result that some dances are almost unrecognisable. One change is the simplification in the dress of the girl dancers, although they possibly cost much more than the dress we had to wear – a heavy kilt, sporran, black velvet or *barathea* jacket and a thick balmoral over a white blouse with five rows of fluted lace.

I loved Highland dancing (and most other dances) for its own sake but I didn't like dancing in competitions and exhibitions. I wasn't an outstanding dancer, although both my sisters were, and I didn't win as many prizes as they did; but when alone I loved to practise my dancing, just for the sheer *joie-de-vivre* I got from it.

In those days, there was no such thing as the Welfare State and my father belonged to a small band of people, including a local minister, who ran concerts to raise funds for charities such as the Highland Orphanage, etc. Dad played his pipes and also played for four of our family to dance the various Highland dances at these functions. We were billed as 'The Chisholm Troupe'.

When on the games circuit, the prize list would depend on who was judging and which system they approved. When the famous piper, Angus Macpherson of Invershin was judging the dancing, he very rarely gave a prize to any of our family as I think he and Dad had different ideas about dancing and piping. However when Brigadier Alasdair MacLean of Pennycross was judging he usually gave us a prize. Incidentally, 'Scruff MacLean', as he was affectionately known in the Camerons, was the first Director of the Military Tattoo during the Edinburgh Festival. I used to wonder what he thought of the Army Highland dancers who danced on the Esplanade, and if they matched up to the talented Army dancers of yesteryear.

The piping judges were sometimes the same people who had judged the dancing at the games but the boys won many prizes and could always keep time for dancers, whereas nowadays it seems difficult to find a piper who can keep to the correct tempo for dancers. In the old days at the games the winning piper in the competitions had to play for an exhibition Reel of Tulloch (foursome reel) danced by the winning four in the dancing competitions, usually two women and two men. Today, when listening to the radio, I very rarely hear a selection of Gaelic airs being played by a piper. It is mostly accordionists and Scottish dance bands who play those. Perhaps modern pipers have no interest to play such tunes (and yet a lot of Gaelic songs are based on the 'ground' of a *piobaireachd*). Sometimes modern pipers play popular tunes which are unsuitable for the scale of the pipes. Yesterday's pipers could compete with the best champion pipers in the *ceol mhor* (the classical music of the bagpipe i.e. the *pibroch* or *piobaireachd*) and then could switch in a moment to playing some of those lovely Gaelic airs. Some people say that the *pibrochs* were played in the old days to urge the Highlanders into battle but that is very difficult to believe as most of them are in the form of laments and very slow-moving ('like a musical symphony' as my Dad used to say), whereas men could keep step with a march or strathspey.

Dad and the brothers composed lots of pipe tunes and I often hear some of their compositions being played by Scottish dance bands on the radio. One of them, by my brother Jack, is called 'Walking the Floor' in memory of the many nights he spent walking the floor with his firstborn, trying to hush him to sleep. Many of the old airs my Dad used to play now go under other names, particularly the Gaelic airs to which English words are put which have no connection with the original Gaelic words, e.g., 'The Waters of Kylesku' is put to a Gaelic tune translated as, 'Thinking of Thee' written by a rejected suitor.

Nowadays the tune, 'The Dark Island' is better-known because of the television serial of that name but I heard my father play it on the pipes when I was a child and it was called 'Dr McInnes' Farewell to South Uist' which of course is a less romantic title. We are told that 'The Dark Island' was composed by an accordionist, who certainly made a most beautiful arrangement of the tune.

My memory of the Argyll & Sutherlands marching past their saluting base has been spoilt by the parody on their march-past, originally called 'The Glendaruel Highlanders' but now known as 'Campbelltown Loch I wish you were Whisky'. I heard it described by that name over the tannoy at the Edinburgh Tattoo some years ago, sacrilege! The tune of 'Morning has Broken' is from the air of the Gaelic Christmas carol 'Child in the Manger' composed by Mary MacDonald from Bunessan in the Isle of Mull. Dad used to say that Dvorak stole a Gaelic melody for use in his New World Symphony and told us Dvorak had heard it sung as an Indian lament. However it was reputed to have its origins in the Gaelic 'Macintosh's Lament', being the lament for the Chief of the Clan Macintosh (or MacKintosh) who was killed falling off his horse on the afternoon of his wedding day. The melody was said to have been brought across the Atlantic by the emigrants from the Highlands at the time of the notorious Highland Clearances when the Highland people were cleared off the land to make room for Lowland sheep farmers and their sheep.

CHAPTER 2

Time was more Elastic Then

W HEN I was young, time seemed a much more elastic commodity than it is today and no-one seemed to rush around. Our day was governed by the school bell. "The bell, the bell the B-E-L-L", we chanted on our way to school. The railway and the Rose Street Foundry hooters always sounded at midday and in the evenings we knew the Cathedral bells pealed at six o'clock and the town bells at eight and ten o'clock.

The eight o'clock bells reminded us that time was getting on and it would soon be time to go indoors for the night. If we were still out by the time the ten o'clock bells rang we would get into hot water at home, if not from the policeman who patrolled our beat. Sometimes, when coming home after spending an evening playing 'lido' or knitting in a friend's house a stone's throw from my own, I would be terrified lest I should come across PC Lumsden's plump, rosy, smiling form because his appearance belied his annoyance at seeing young children out late and he would tell us in no uncertain terms that it was time we were home. All the same I don't think the Inverness streets held so many dangers for youngsters as they do today and although we respected the 'Bobbies', we were a wee bit afraid of being on the wrong side of the law.

Perhaps it's just nostalgia for lost youth which always surrounds my childhood days in Innes Street with an aura of sunshine, music and laughter. Certainly the sheer joy of roller-skating or running barefoot up and down the flat, even concrete pavement was a thrilling experience on a hot summer's day ... but were those hot summer days as numerous as my memory suggests?

It's a pity no-one has gathered all the Inverness children's street-play, songs and rhymes of the 1930s, as they appear to be that little bit different from other parts of Scotland. For instance, I had never heard of the game of 'peevers' (hopscotch) as played in the Lowlands of Scotland until I grew up and realised that they were a form of our 'beddies' which we played with 'skeetchies' made from glazed tiles which we found outside the fireplace store near the Rose Street Foundry. While we searched for 'skeetchies' there, the boys gathered the round metallic shilling-like offcuts from the machines and clinked them in their pockets to make believe they had money to jingle.

Invernessians are well known for adding 'ee' or 'ie' to the end of familiar words in an endearing fashion, for instance, the 'old wifie' or 'wee mannie' or 'Bakie's Shoppie'. 'Bakie's Shoppie' was our equivalent of the modern teenage cafe. The owner was Miss Rebecca MacKay who served groceries to our parents and mouth-watering sweets and worldly-wise advice to us. It was considered the height of sophistication to sit on an upturned crate in Bakie's sucking a Barratt's sherbert fountain through a liquorice straw, watching the world going by.

There never seemed to be a dull moment in our street and the residents themselves were a varied collection. Most of them were long-suffering as far as children's noise was concerned but there were some who did not like children (often those with no children themselves). They made a point of keeping any ball which happened to fall into their pocket-handkerchief front gardens. However, the boys meted out rough justice by waiting until it was dark, tying a string to the knocker or one of the large jangling bell-pulls and then keeping up regular door-knocking or bell-ringing until they wore out their victims.

At midday and in the evenings the street would be thronged with 'black spots', moving three and four abreast down the street and making for the Black Bridge, as we called the Waterloo Bridge. Those would be men in dungarees going home from work at the Railway or Foundry workshops. What cheery fellows they seemed to be in those days of hard work, long hours, no works canteens and low wages. They never passed us without a word of greeting or giving us a cigarette card of our favourite film stars.

At Hallowe'en time, every door was open to us (except for the few meanies like the ball-keeping ones and other odd-bods) but we had to work for our nuts and apples. None of us stood dumb on the doorstep or on the floor, waiting for the handouts without giving anything in return. We planned our 'turns' and disguises weeks beforehand.

We even gave what we called 'concerts' in our back garden, which was hardly a garden, merely a back green shared by our neighbours. My father rigged up a stage (a large wooden square platform) for us and many a budding trouper showed his or her paces there, accompanied by cries of encouragement or derisive catcalls from the critical audience. Although our concert would be packed full, the entrance fee was nominal, more-or-less as a token. I remember paying two pins as an entrance fee to view a showing of a Laurel and Hardy film on a cinematograph owned by one of my brother's friends. At the time, it never occurred to me to wonder what he did with the thirty or so pins he received ... unless his mother was a keen dressmaker or practised acupuncture!

There was an open space at the foot of George Street which backed on and ran parallel to Innes Street and we used to play there, in what we called the 'Parkie'. This was our training ground for sledging until we graduated to the slopes of Culcabock golf course when we were older and anyway, council houses were built on the Parkie by then. The Cresta Run had nothing on the run down the golf course brae; all the more thrilling when it ended with a 'dook' in the burn. At that time it seemed as if the whole of Inverness resorted to the golf course with sledges in winter. Sometimes we would go to *Loch-na-Sanais* (now within the bounds of the Torvean golf course) when it was frozen over, and it was there that I learned the horrible truth that I could never balance my weight on ice-skates, although I could roar up and down the street on roller-skates quite expertly.

John Gilpin's ride to York could not have been more exciting than the ride I remember in my push-chair, down the hill from some farm, where the farmer had caught some Innes Street children in his turnip field – and I still love raw turnip. Although I would have been under school age at the time, I still remember it vividly.

Although everyone had room at the back of their houses to play, children are very gregarious and we preferred to play in the street. Sometimes we would have to stop our street games because of a procession of horses, each with a long, low wooden trailer on wheels as long as a modern articulated lorry, on which there was balanced a long tree trunk like a telegraph pole. This procession went at a snail's pace and was headed for the sawmill in Shore Street. The boys used to enjoy the ride down the street at the side of the driver or at the back of the trailer.

One of the boys' favourites was Charlie the Drover, who drove the sheep and cattle down the street to their doom in the slaughterhouse at the Citadel, to be made into mince, sausages and 'trollybags' (the name we used for the sheep's udders which were used for making black and white puddings and haggis etc.). The boys thought it was a great event to 'help' Charlie when a runaway bull had to be chased around the Longman and down our street again. As for me, I felt safer with the front door between me and any likely Ferdinand. I was amused to read, years later, of the runaway bull which mounted the stairs in the old Buttercup Dairy premises in Hamilton Street (now occupied by Marks & Spencer).

The boys liked to 'help' all sorts of people – like the staff at Alan Cobham's Air Circus on the Longman Aerodrome when they came to town and charged 2/6d for an air flight. My brothers had their share of 'looping-the-loop' for nothing, in return for odd jobs round the aerodrome.

The Longman: what scenes that name conjures up for me! It was our favourite picnic spot and, on a fine day, most of the mothers in the street brought their children there to swim, collect mussels and winkles or play around a crackling twig fire until the tea was ready. In those days there was only the golf course on the Longman and some shooting butts (I think for the Territorial Army) and the airfield. There were no industrial buildings as there are today. We could start off from the bottom of Innes Street and walk all around the Longman and come by the top of the street without meeting a car.

At night the Longman would become transformed from the bright playground into an eerie, frightening place, particularly near the haunted house. This was a ruined dwelling house near Seafield Farm and probably got its name because it was derelict and the moonlight threw weird shadows from the trees around it. I was too terrified to go near it even in broad daylight.

I have often puzzled over the origin of the name, the Longman, and wonder if there was any truth in the answer given me by one of the older girls when I asked about it. She said it was so called because there was an outlaw buried there and that his grave stretched all the way round, as he had been so long – hence the 'long man'. She even pointed out a large stone at the corner of a drystone dyke facing the sea and said that that was the gravestone and that a nearby tree was where the outlaw had been hanged. In later years when I began to think about it, I wondered if this could possibly have been my Hebridean grandmother's bogeyman, namely 'Mac-an-t-Srònaich', notorious Lewis outlaw. We always spent our school holidays on the Island of Lewis in the Outer Hebrides and, when we were out of hand, Granny would threaten us with 'Mac-an-Stronaich'. Granny told us hair-raising stories of the outlaw's escapades and said he was a mass-murderer who had lived in a cave near the village and, sometimes when he was hungry, he would come down at night to steal children and eat them! From what I could gather in later years there was an outlaw of that name whose real name was supposedly MacKenzie (although some said it was Cameron because the Gaelic name is similar to the word for Cameron), but it doesn't necessarily follow that the outlaw's name was patronymic and it could have been a nickname. He was supposed to have come from the Gairloch area and had escaped to the Hebrides where he had committed several murders in the Lewis/Harris area. Eventually, he seems to have been outwitted, captured and hanged in Inverness and buried … but whereabouts no-one seems to know, unless perhaps he was really the 'long man'.

The ragman was always a welcome visitor to our street. We scrounged around for rags and woollens in exchange for goldfish, balloons and whirring birds on gaily coloured sticks. Sometimes the exchange rates were cups and saucers – very dull alternatives to our minds. We had the regular beggars too, called after their line of patter or appearance, for instance, 'Spare a copper' or 'Forty pockets'. We were all warned of the consequence of calling after tramps and the like and told that we would be gobbled up by bears like the children in the Bible who had called after the prophet Elisha. That warning did not deter some of the more impudent boys.

There was music in our street too, supplied by those buskers who wandered around looking for money. Some of them certainly earned their fee. They were the most colourful visitors to our street, which was popular, perhaps it was because it was long and broad with plenty of room for improvisation and wide pavements for the audience. Some of them could put on a good show, to our unsophisticated eyes.

There was one old couple who regularly toured the street, he with an orange box which he placed down lovingly for his wife to sit on, while he sang in a quavering voice 'Rock of Ages' or 'In the good old Summertime', his wife sometimes joining in with him. They were both a source of inspiration for my young brother and sister, who used to imitate them when playing at home in the evenings.

There was a roly-poly of a wee mannie who was a wizard on the spoons. He made a clickitty-clackitty click-click noise all up and down his arms, legs and thighs and then he would turn somersaults, periodically singing. His forté was, 'Oh, I wonder, yes, I wonder, will the angels way up yonder, will the angels play their harps for me?' I wonder! In passing it occurs to me that everyone seemed to be singing in my young days: mothers at the sink, children with linked arms coming down the street and the errand boys and workmen all whistled and sang as they went about their business. I rarely hear folks singing nowadays when they're going out and about.

There was another fellow who plonkitty-plonk plonked and twanged his Jew's (or Jaws) Harp and another who accompanied his ditties with the cracking of ivory sticks stuck between each of his fingers. One of my brothers used to plunder the soup-leftovers for flank bones which he dried off and made 'crackers' which he played quite successfully.

The busker who annoyed us most was the violinist who scraped jerkily at his violin in the early hours of Sunday morning before breakfast, when we were trying to enjoy a long lie. There seemed to be no tune in the sound he was making and yet, when I later came to appreciate music properly, I could detect a faint resemblance in his staccato-like playing to 'Humoresque'. It could be that he was a professional violinist down on his luck.

My own favourite busker was 'Cappie Eppie'. I think the 'Cappie' part must have been *à la* Invernessian for the hip length cape she wore over her long black skirt; or perhaps the huge golfer's cap she sometimes wore. Her whole appearance, as I remember, resembled that of the 'Old Mother Riley' character created for the film of that name around the thirties – but I don't know who copied whom. Sometimes she wore a black mutch affair tied with black ribbons under her chin. She played a melodeon but I cannot remember her playing any particular tune. All I remember was that I could never keep my feet still when I heard her playing and kicking my legs up in time to the music. I got into lots of trouble for scuffing my school shoes imitating her antics. I was very upset one day to see poor Cappie lying in the gutter, face-downwards, clutching her melodeon. I thought she was dead. However one of the grown-ups who knew all told me not to worry as she wasn't dead; just dead drunk. The story goes that she had been from a good family and had become addicted to the bottle.

I don't know what happened to Cappie and the other buskers who came to our street, because we moved away to a new house further away from the town centre, where they didn't visit, perhaps because they wouldn't have got such an appreciative audience. No doubt the Welfare State takes care of most of the 'Cappie Eppies' and 'Forty Pockets' of this generation and yet I've seen the dropouts recently when passing through London and they are just as featured in the song, 'Streets of London'. They look miserable compared to the happy-go-lucky 'fellows who don't fit in' of my childhood years.

My daughters laugh when I tell them that from the age of around twelve, any boy known to us would never pass on the street without saluting or touching his cap – even if we hated the sight of each other!

We just nodded our heads slightly, smiled and passed on our way, especially if either of us were accompanied with a grown-up.

At the school dance, no-one would stand in front of us with a hitch-hiking style 'thumbs up' and take it for granted that we knew he was asking us to dance. Such a request was always preceded with a little bow and a, "May I?" More hoots of derision when I tell my daughters about the little cards with pencils attached which we wore on our wrists for very special dances. To this, they ask, did I really grow up in the Victorian age? Contrasting present day standards, I just smile wistfully and think I'd never trade their so-called 'modern' styles for my childhood days of 'gracious living' now, alas, gone with the wind!

I'd say there seemed to be a spirit of camaraderie among the parents and children of Innes Street. Except for the odd snob, there was no 'keeping up with the Joneses'. Sometimes, on a visit to Inverness, I make a special pilgrimage down Innes Street but, like everywhere else, there are no 'characters' to be seen and it is only when I meet up with childhood friends that Innes Street comes alive once more.

CHAPTER 3

Mum and Dad

THERE is a Gaelic song called, '*Mo Mhathair*' (My Mother) which is often sung on the radio and played by Scottish dance bands as a waltz. Whenever I hear it sung, I think of my own mother. My mother was the epitome of the word 'Mother' and I expect was typical of most mothers of that day. She lived a life of unselfish devotion to her husband and children and I used to think privately that it was too much so and that I wouldn't be tied to the house as she seemed to be. Yet, she always appeared happy and contented and she was placid by nature, whereas my father had an exuberant personality.

We called my mother 'Ma', 'Mammy', 'Mum' or sometimes 'Mother' and she always seemed to have time to listen to our hopes and fears. She very rarely went out in the evenings except occasionally to visit friends. On the other hand, there was no need to look far for companionship as our house always seemed full of friends and neighbours who called Mum 'Chis' unless they were Hebrideans who called her by her Gaelic name Shonnag (Johan). Mum must have been a very good manager, as I don't ever remember having to do without food or clothing and it surprises me to remember that, when we needed new shoes, we were brought to the best shoe shop in town to be fitted. Although she used to alter outgrown clothes to suit the younger members of the family, she didn't believe in handed-down shoes that the older children had worn and we always had our own new shoes. I used to like the black lacing shoes I wore with the heel shaped like a cam-shaft to keep my feet level supposedly but, in spite of wearing those shoes, I still seem to wear my heels down on one side. Except for a day here and there and perhaps a visit to friends in Nairn or Aberdeen or Fortrose, we didn't go away for Easter or Christmas holidays but summer holidays saw us all off to the Isle of Lewis where we spent some of the happiest days of our young lives. Mum made most of our clothes – sometimes even our kilt outfits which were painstakingly sewn up by her on her machine and she knitted our tartan kilt socks. Nowadays these items seem to cost a fortune.

Mum never used a pattern for her knitting. She could look at a piece of knitting and copy it. She made beautiful Shetland shawls for all her grandchildren and her own long cambric christening gown with *broderie anglaise* was always kept fresh and starched, ready for the grandchildren's christenings. Our balmorals (the flat berets, not the Glengarry type shaped like a forage cap) for us younger ones were usually made out of ordinary Basque berets with petersham binding and ribbons hanging down the back and a hand-made pompom of red wool (called a 'toorie') on top. She sometimes made our school blazers when we were small and she bound them with coloured braid but my gym frocks were always bought. Mum was always kept busy knitting jerseys for the boys, as they were very careless about catching them on fences, etc. and, more often than not, Alex and Jack would come home with yards of wool hanging from their sleeves where they had caught on something or where someone else had frayed them.

We always had home-made scones but very rarely had shop cakes (we called them 'Dainties') until the time came when we were earning and there was more money to go around. I never left the table hungry and Mum's soup and stew was always full of vegetables from Dad's plot. He leased the plot from the Railway Company near his office, where he worked as a Stores Clerk.

Chis was the 'Enquire Within' of the neighbours and they would come in to ask her opinion about some problem. Although she didn't have much spare time she liked reading and always made time to read the papers. Our house always had bookcases full of books on all subjects. There was no order in the bookcases and I remember a

Life of Schubert right up against *The Coral Island* with Ian Hay's *The First Hundred Thousand* on the other side. Mum's *Medical Dictionary* used to be borrowed quite often until she discovered that one of her neighbours had started imagining that she had serious illness because her symptoms seemed to resemble various diseases … so Mum refused to lend Mrs F the book any more, as she thought it would lead to Mrs F's thinking that she had every disease in the book.

There was never a bare cupboard in our house and I never heard my parents arguing about money. My father didn't have a big wage but he had an army pension, having been a regular soldier for many years and only retired shortly before I was born in 1919. Perhaps the money went further, I don't know, but we all understood that, while there was enough money for the necessities of life, there wasn't much for luxuries and we didn't worry overmuch about that when we were small. At Christmas time our stockings were filled by Santa Claus. There would be a toy or perhaps two, some sweets, an apple and a tangerine wrapped in silver paper and one or two items of clothing which we hadn't to wear until New Year's Day, on our trip to a matinee at the 'pictures' (cinema). It would be only on rare occasions that we went to the cinema during the rest of the year. When we grew up and visited home we still hung up our stockings on Christmas Eve so that the others would fill it – and they usually did, except that my brothers – Callum and Ian – always included lumps of coal or sausages in mine!

In our younger days, a lot of Hebridean girls used to come to the mainland to work as nurses or domestics and some of them came to Inverness, although most went to Glasgow. There was always a welcome for them in our house and we regularly had them visit for tea. I used to go to the hall where their coats were hung, close my eyes and, taking their Harris Tweed coats in my hand, lift them up to my nose and snuggle into them. The peat reek always seemed to linger on the tweed and I'd be transported back to my favourite Isle of Lewis which I thought of as '*Tir-nan-Og*' (The Land of the Ever-Young or the Gael's Paradise).

I wonder now at my mother's ability to produce a meal and a bed for anyone out of the blue, so to speak. Mum bought some groceries from Bakie and her fresh eggs from Miss Gordon at the top of the street as she belonged to Gairloch and had the best eggs. I had a little basket like a miniature hamper which I used on the occasions I went to Miss Gordon's. The bulk of our groceries were sent by the Co-operative, all tied up with brown paper and string in a horse-drawn van. There was also a horse-drawn milk van and a baker's van. Our favourite baker was Anderson in Academy Street. What a variety of loaves they sold – plain, turnover, pan, French, Vienna, milk and cottage loaves – but my favourite was their huge cabin biscuits with lashings of butter and thick slices of cheddar cheese. Sometimes I had to go to MacGillivray's butchers shop on Chapel Street for sausages and sausage meat. I have to confess that I sometimes took a wee corner off the sausage meat on my way home and ate it – YUCK (or, as Invernessians say, 'GYADDIES')!

Every Saturday night for tea we had a huge clootie dumpling (like a steamed fruit pudding made in a cloth instead of a bowl) which we called a 'plum duff', followed by an outsize apple pie. They were very filling but Ian used to call the dumpling, 'Cheat the Belly' as he felt too full at table to eat as much as he wanted and then, half an hour later, his appetite returned in full force, once the table was cleared. The boys played football and I played hockey on Saturdays and we raced home for our tea. There used to be a simple sort of fellow who lived in the local Poorhouse and, if my mother saw him walking down our street on a Saturday evening, she would invite him in to join the throng and he always seemed to enjoy Mum's cooking and our company. The boys used to say it was a shame that he was always dressed in 'Poorhouse Tweed', but it was good quality tweed (perhaps Harris Tweed) and probably kept him warmer than grey flannel. The brothers could never understand how Mum could put up with the neighbouring children who would pop into the house just to watch her at work or to sit on the fender-stools and tell her about their doings. There were two particular wee girls – Connie and Peggy – from different neighbouring homes, who always seemed to hog the fireside seats. Jack used to be annoyed with them and teased them mercilessly, but I think it was all a front as he was really quite fond of them. He used to make fun of Peggy, an only child, when she would say to Mum, "Chis – listen to my wheeze" and Jack would accuse her of 'putting on the agony' but Mum would sympathise with the wee girl. Sometimes she really had a wheeze in her chest but, at other times, she would whistle herself to gain Mum's sympathy.

It's a mystery to me how anyone can cope with a family of ten children, although half had left home before the other half reached their teenage years. When I was aged ten, in 1929, my eldest brother Angus sailed for India with the Queen's Own Cameron Highlanders. How did Mum manage all the washing, ironing, etc? I used to be exhausted coping with five children. I think I must have been a very thoughtless child as I don't remember ever worrying about all the work Mum had to do – I just took it for granted that my clean clothes and meals would be there when I wanted them.

Sometimes, particularly when there was a new baby in the house, Mum would have help by way of Annie Murchison, a little woman from the Kyle of Lochalsh area who spoke Gaelic with (to me) a 'funny' accent. I don't expect she charged much for her services but she went around to various houses, helping when necessary. She sometimes wore a striped outfit like a nurse (perhaps she had done some nurse training) but her role was just a 'Mother's Help' and my elder sister told me she used to stop working very often and say "It's time for a cup of tea". She once said we should call her Nurse but we called her 'Miss Murchison' when we spoke to her and 'Annie Murch' when we spoke among ourselves. We were always taught to respect our elders and I was really sorry for my brother Alex when he got a row at home when one of the street 'scaffies' (our name for street sweepers and binmen) complained to my father that Alex had called names after him. When the matter was investigated it was found that what Alex had said was, "Hullo, Mr Meechie Mahoony". He sometimes visited our home and was well known for praying at the Church and in homes, so poor Alex thought that he was giving him his title, whereas it was the phonetic sound of his Gaelic nickname 'Praying Murdo'. I don't know if 'Meechie' appreciated my father's explanation but it gave us all a good laugh. I may say that, having spent most of my school holidays and eight years of my retirement in Lewis, I am sometimes at a loss to know the correct surnames of some of the locals as they are more widely known by their nicknames. One evening my mother brought me to visit Annie Murchison in her one-roomed flat in Church Street and I was astounded to see that the room contained very little except two cabin trunks and wooden boxes. Perhaps she didn't spend much time there during her working life. Annie continued to visit us long after her services were no longer required and had the bad habit of overstaying her welcome, sometimes until around midnight. My Dad didn't want to hurt her feelings but he would pointedly start winding the mantelpiece clock and this rather tactless hint thrown out by Dad would remind Annie of the late hour. During the war Annie would appear in the blackout with a huge lantern instead of a torch, which created great hilarity in our family as it was like the lanterns one used to see porters carrying on railway stations at night. Even after we all had homes of our own, Annie continued to visit us and, at Christmas time, she doled out a threepenny piece to each of our children, just as she had done to their parents in the past. Annie had a good sense of humour and, although she could take a joke at her own expense from her friends, I've seen her giving back as good measure to another of our visitors and that in a very subtle manner.

I never heard my mother grumbling about her lot in life. She took everything in her stride and never seemed to be depressed but always looked on the bright side. When I suffer any hardship or a knock in life, I think my mother must have passed something of her philosophy to me as I feel there is always someone worse off than I am and then I count my blessings. My mother was a tall woman, well built with long black hair, which she wore in 'earphones' – plaited round each ear – or plaited like a wreath right round her head. She had a graceful carriage which was so unlike my round-shouldered stoop. I remember when I had my first child and she visited me in hospital, the nurses said she looked like a Duchess. She had a kind of dignified walk and manner and never seemed in a hurry.

Although Mother sang us the lullabies when we were children, it was my Dad who told us the stories – long, short and sometimes very tall stories. Mum was a quiet, gentle, placid person. Dad, on the other hand, was gregarious and liked nothing better than having friends round to engage in lively conversation and story-telling.

I suppose, in Highland parlance my Father would have been called a 'blether'. If he was one, then that was not much of a bad thing as I learnt much through his 'blethers' and our house was always the venue for friendly, neighbourly foregatherings at which anything could be discussed, from the origin of the name Tomnahurich (Gaelic '*Tom-na-h-iubraich*' for 'The hill of the Yew Trees') to the German's latest secret weapon. There never seemed to be a lull in the conversation when Dad was around. The only person I ever heard out-talking my Dad was a London-based uncle of my mother's who had a limitless supply of yarns to tell of the days when he had been to sea and around 'The world that's full of wonders'. Of course Dad had been around a lot of the world, starting from the day when he joined the Seaforth Highlanders Militia at fifteen years old (using his elder brother's birth certificate to enlist), then transferring to the Cameron Highlanders under his own name. I remember wondering why, in the Army group photographs on the wall of our stairs, my father's name was listed as 'Duncan Chisholm' and, on the other, as 'Malcolm Chisholm'; but it was only when I grew up I was told the reason. Dad used to say that the English (or southern Scots) officers couldn't get their tongues round his name and used to call him 'Mol-column Chis-holm'. However, in the Army he was always known as 'Bill Chisholm' and I noticed recently in some of the volumes of the Transactions of the Gaelic Society of Inverness, to which Dad was the Honorary Piper, he is named as 'William Chisholm'. To his own family and Gaelic-speaking friends he was known by his Gaelic name of Callum.

Although Dad told tales of fighting the Dervishes and having to march all the way from Capetown to the Sudan during the Sudan War, most of the stories he told had a Hebridean flavour. All the same, he must have had a gruelling time during the South African War, as he was present with Kitchener's Army at the Battle of Atbara on 8th April 1898. One of the prints hanging on our stairway was of the 1st Battalion Seaforth Highlanders charging the Zareba, supported by the fire of the 1st Battalion of the Queen's Own Cameron Highlanders, through a gap in whose ranks they passed in the midst of the battle. One of the other prints was the one of Piper Findlater, of the Gordon Highlanders, sitting on a rock during the Battle for the Heights of Dargai, India, as a result of which he won the Victoria Cross. I used to hear my brothers singing a ditty to the tune of 'Cock o' the North' (The Gordon Highlanders' March Past). "Piper Findlay, Piper Findlay won the Victoria Cross. When he was shot he sat on a rock and played 'The Cock o' the North'". One of my brothers has the set of pipes my Dad played during the Battle of Atbara, where he was wounded on the chin and he bore the scar throughout his life. His tales didn't throw any heroic light on himself, although he had several campaign medals which are now in the Highlanders Museum in Fort George. Dad was a fanatic as far as the Cameron Highlanders were concerned and we all held 'The Regiment' in a special place in our hearts. After the Second World War, General Montgomery said he thought it would be better to do away with local Regiments and their 'Tribal Traditions' (as he put it) but where would he have been at the Battle of El Alamein without the Highland Division? Dunkirk might have been a worse disaster when France turned tail and left the Fifty-First Highland Division to fight a rearguard action at St Valery-en-Caux, resulting in their incarceration in prisoner-of-war camps for the remainder of the war. Of course I think it was Pitt who said that Highlanders were 'expendable' while praising their fighting qualities! At the end of this chapter is a poem I wrote at the time in response to General Montgomery's assertion that it would be better to dispense with the 'Tribal Traditions' of the local regiments.

Dad's stories were mostly amusing but they bored us, as we heard them told over and over again to his cronies and we treated some of his tales with an element of scepticism. Perhaps the most celebrated close-shave story was that of Corporal Lawrie of the 1st Battalion Seaforth Highlanders who earned the nickname of the 'bullet-proof man'. He was first hit by a bullet which took the toecap off his left boot but, as the boot had been too big for easy marching and sleeping at night, it missed his foot. Then a bullet bent his bayonet at right angles. A third went through his left sleeve by the wrist, making two holes in the cloth but without touching him. A fourth splintered the butt of his rifle as he was loading. A spear thrown by a Dervish in a trench split his haversack, but missed his ribs by an inch. Another bullet at last grazed the back of his hand slightly. Finally, as he reached the edge of the dried-up river Atbara beyond the 'Dem', a bullet fired from the river bed below him hit his right ammunition pouch, passed through his right pocket breaking two pencils and smashing his penknife, tore his shirt in four places and scratched his chest for three inches, emerging from his jacket through his equipment brace by his left shoulder. When we raised our eyebrows at this story, Dad told us that Corporal Lawrie's letter home was published in 'The Scotsman' in 'Black and White', as Dad said, which always seemed to authenticate any tall tale. We never heard what happened to the 'bullet-proof man' in the same way as we never heard what happened to 'John Lee – the man they couldn't hang' – another of Dad's yarns.

Although we would try to hide our boredom as we heard a story being re-told for the benefit of a visitor who had never heard it, we all wish we had listened more to the tales Dad told as there was a wealth of folklore and tradition in them. He spent quite a lot of time browsing and delving in old Gaelic and Celtic literature and music and subscribed to several magazines and periodicals which published those articles.

Stories were not necessarily told in the evenings or at bedtime. Mostly, it would be an association of ideas which suggested a tale to Dad. Anyone dreading a visit to the dentist might be treated to the story of 'Finn's Tooth of Knowledge', so that the horror of the dentist's chair would be forgotten for a while in the wonder of the tale. We would sometimes ask to be told a story, and the reply would be, "I'll tell you a story about Johnnie Glory (surely a forerunner of 'Jackanory' on television), if you don't speak in the middle of it. Will you?" On our answering "No", he would say, "There now, you've spoken". He would repeat the question once or twice, probably a preliminary to ensure that he got our full attention before embarking on the story.

Being the son of the croft and raised in the Isle of Lewis, my father was very interested in the cause of the crofters' struggle to secure rights to their land. He avidly read and retained many press articles about the crofters' uprisings in Skye and Lewis covered in both local and national press. The crofters' uprisings resulted in many crofters being imprisoned for protesting against unfair practices of 'tyrannical' landlords and the Congested Districts Board.

Daddy was also a keen gardener. The available space in our back green was shared by our neighbours for washing lines and all that grew there was a small patch of grass, a pear tree, an apple tree and a gorgeously-scented purple lilac tree near the back door. There had once been gooseberry bushes but Dad had cut them down after a boy down the street had died, supposedly, from gorging himself with green gooseberries from his own garden. Dad's vegetables were grown in the allotment he leased from his employers – the London, Midland and Scottish Railway Company – and there was plenty of room to grow vegetables there, just round a corner at the bottom of Innes Street. Dad was especially proud of his giant cabbages and the marrows he grew, but my Mum used to tease him as he would never bring home his biggest cabbage but left it in the plot till the last. He wasn't interested in entering any of his produce for the shows or exhibitions but enjoyed bringing home the vegetables in his punnet. His lettuce was a treat in the summer evenings when we were called in for bed, as Mum used to put them in a huge crystal bowl with cut-up tomatoes which we had with our bedtime cup of 'Lutona' cocoa. There used to be coupons in the cocoa tin which Mum gave to me to save and I'd send them off to the CWS at Luton in exchange for a box of chocolates. Sometimes I'd go down to Dad's plot with him and then he would bring me into his office and give me one of his notebooks. This was like a shorthand notebook but covered in red linen cloth and had a brass clasp for closing it. I used to sit on a high stool while Dad caught up with some extra work and I'd admire the row of brass paper-clips shaped like a woman's hand with a dainty imitation lace frilled cuff, holding up requisition forms.

Dad was the Pipe Major of the Inverness British Legion Pipe Band and we loved to go up to town on the evenings in the summer when they played through the streets and marched out to the Ness Islands where they performed. There would be multi-coloured lights strung on the trees in the Islands and there would be a concert held in a small open-air arena where we sometimes gave exhibition dances. In another area in the Islands there was a huge open-air stage where couples could pay one shilling to do modern dancing to a dance band. When it rained too heavily the fêtes (as they were called) were cancelled.

Mum and Dad worked as a team and shared the responsibilities of the home, Mum doing the housework and cooking and Dad cutting the sticks, bringing in the coal, mending the shoes and repairing the furniture etc. He used to get off-cuts of leather through his work and made beautifully soft dancing pumps for us. He used to buy sleepers from the railway and store them in the shed and then cut them on the trestle and chop them up for kindling. There was no problem in igniting the fire with those as they were saturated with creosote.

My parents had a wonderful sense of humour and they were full of fun and I think, as a family we inherited this. Dad used to make up songs about some topical event or about one of the local characters. Mostly those would be in Gaelic but, alas, although he could read and speak his native Gaelic language, he couldn't write it properly and used to ask my Lewis cousin Nina to correct his spelling before giving it to me to type when I was older. Dad told us that, when he went to school on the Isle of Lewis, Gaelic was a forbidden language in the playground and, if any of the children forgot this, they would be whacked by the teacher. When he was abroad he kept up his love of the language by arranging to have Gaelic magazines sent to him and I still have one or two of them with his name, rank and Army number on the flyleaf. Dad would sing his Gaelic compositions to his friends and would sometimes say in Gaelic, "*Sea mi fheinn a rin e*" ("It's myself who made it") and we would quote this *sotto voce* to each other. However my brother Ken turned the tables on Dad when presenting Jean, the first grandchild. Dad adored her on first sight and Ken just said to him in Gaelic, after hearing words of admiration from Dad, "It's myself who made her". One of the funniest songs I remember typing out for Dad was one about returning from holiday in Lewis with a full case containing, among other things, a home-made black pudding which an old woman had given him to take home. Unfortunately, the pudding began to smell (who knows how old it was!) and Dad couldn't find the key of the case with the result that it was an embarrassment all the way on the steamer and train, causing him many awkward moments.

It must have been a hard struggle for Mum and Dad to bring up ten children but we were never aware of it being so. Although we knew that we couldn't afford to go on school trips to Paris and Brussels, there were few others who could afford such trips in those days, despite the cost being only around ten pounds apiece. Our 'extra' pounds were always put aside for holiday fares, etc. and we probably benefited more from the fresh Hebridean air than from being cooped up in a city. We were brought up with a good mixture of love and self-discipline which I don't think any of us felt the worse for and, when time came to make a career, we all fell into our own niche in life, with freedom of choice.

I often find myself using the same phrases to my children as my parents used to me. When we asked Dad for permission to do something out of the ordinary, he wouldn't agree or disagree immediately. He would say, "We shall see what we shall see". Another expression he used was 'Corn in Egypt' which was applied to us if we were 'flush' with money. This phrase is taken from the Bible but in a different context!

Mum used to say, "When he/she's tired, he/she'll stop", when we complained about another member of the family teasing us. Another of Mum's sayings was, "Waste not, want not", and she would never allow us to throw a crumb or food into the fire saying, "There are thousands of children starving". If we were naughty, Mum sometimes called us a 'garron' which I understand now means a Highland pony with a reputation for being very stubborn.

Reply to Montgomery

Christina wrote this verse in response to Field Marshal Montgomery, once a Commander and admirer of the 5th (Scottish) and 51st (Highland) Divisions, who later declared that such 'Tribal Traditions' of the regiments should be disbanded (to be sung to tune 'March of The Cameron Men').

We don't like your jibe at the Cameron 'tribe'
With their kilts and their hackles of blue;
And what were your fate at El Alamein's Gate
If they hadn't all fought around you?

But should you hear the war-cry resounding
I know you would want all those men.
You'd put on your battledress and your beret
And call them all down from the glen –
Your 'tribesmen' – our clansmen –
To fight in your wars once again.

When battle is o'er and peace reigns once more
You will wave them goodbye with a smile
Loudly singing their praises; but then, as before,
You'll forget all that in a short while..

Or until you hear the war-drums a-pounding
Then you will remember those men.
You'll put on your battledress and your beret
And call them all down from the glen –
Your 'tribesmen' – our clansmen –
To fight in your wars once again …

Would you send to perdition that 'tribal tradition'
Which uplifted hearts in the field
Could you silence that shout in the midst of the rout
'A Cameron never can yield?'

Then you hear the war-torn pibroch a-sounding
You'll call those sons of the glen
And isn't it true "What men dare they can do"
And they'll die by your side once again –
Your 'tribesmen' – our clansmen –
Those loyal, brave Cameron men!

C.J.M.

CHAPTER 4

The Magnificent Seven

THERE were no brothers like my brothers, as far as I was concerned and I wasn't in the least surprised when some of my school friends fell in love with at least one of them.

My parents kept up the old Highland traditions as far as possible in the way of giving children family names. The first son was always called after a grandfather and my eldest brother was called after my mother's father; Angus MacPhail. The next brother was called Kenneth after my father's father. The rest all had family names. I was told that there was an uproar during the choosing of my brother Callum's name – Malcolm – as my father wanted him called 'Torquil MacLeod Chisholm' after Dad's maternal grandfather who had been one of the 'Siol Torcuil' ('The seed of Torquil') – the Chiefs of the MacLeods of Lewis. Although Mum probably wouldn't have minded, the older members of the family thought it was too unusual a name for a child as they had never heard it and they made such a furore (one crying over it) that it was decided to name the child after his own father. Callum often used to quote, "Call him what you call him but 'Callum is MY name'".

I used to think I could divide my brothers by their likenesses to different sides of the family, for instance, some were Chisholms and some were MacPhails, but as they grew older, they seemed to change from one side to the other and the brothers whom I thought resembled the Macphails suddenly appeared to be Chisholms. My elder sister was definitely a Chisholm when she was young, with dark brown eyes and black hair whereas I was a MacPhail with grey-blue eyes and fair hair but, as we grew older, we looked quite alike.

My brother Angus was always the boss. He could be a real tormentor and yet, underneath, he had a heart of gold. When he returned home after six years in India with the Camerons, I didn't recognise him on returning from school and thought he was a 'Silkada Jump', which was Invernessian for the Indians who came round with suitcases selling silk jumpers etc. from India.

Having been born and brought up at Cameron Barracks in Inverness, Angus was steeped in regimental lore. Although when he left school he started as a draughtsman-apprentice with the Rose Street Foundry (afterwards Resistance Welders who made the PLUTO – Pipe Line under the Ocean – during the Second World War), his heart was with the Camerons and, when he became old enough, he joined up. He used to sing barrack songs and, when I pass the statue of the kilted Highlander on Inverness Station Square, I often imagine I hear Angus singing, "Remember Allan Cameron and those who fell so dear – first in the fight for God and right at Tel-el-Kebir". He told me that the statue was modelled on a man from the Isle of Harris known to Dad. Most of Angus's service was spent in India and Africa and he lost his left eye in the Libyan Campaign during WWII. He kept in touch with us, sending most interesting letters and photos which, in those days, were wonderful to us. He had a 'Standing Order' from Paddy to bring him three things when he came home – a parrot, a snake and a monkey. When he did come home on furlough, he brought lots of Indian handiwork but no parrot, snake or monkey. The customs were to blame, he said. What I did enjoy was his huge photograph album, covered in Cameron of Erracht tartan, full of snapshots of dancing bears and the temple where monkeys were worshipped, the Taj Mahal, the Indian Pipe Bands which Angus taught, several personal ones of the Cameron Pipe Band, one of Angus riding an elephant and another on his horse playing polo. The other book I coveted was a large ledger-sized book, full of scraps of interesting facts, poems and songs which were handwritten by Angus. I don't know what happened to that book but I know there was a lot of Kipling in it and some regimental history, including Lady Ashmore's 'Sonnet to the Cameron Men' and Mary Maxwell Campbell's 'The March of the Cameron Men', one verse of which used to move me to tears:

> *Oh, proudly they walk but each Cameron knows*
> *He may tread on the heather no more*
> *But boldly he follows his Chief to the field*
> *Where his laurels were gathered before.*

The last verse of 'The Cameron Men' says:

> *High, high are their hopes, for their Chieftain hath said*
> *That whatever men dare they can do.*

The words, 'Whatever men dare ...' were taken and used in a recruiting manual for the Camerons with a photograph of my brother Angus and the story of his service in the Regiment. After recovering in hospital from his wounds, Angus was posted to India. For a time he was an Aide-de-Camp to General Wavell whom he had known in Egypt and, when Wavell was recalled, Angus was posted to a branch of the Ministry of Economic Warfare (which Churchill called 'The Ministry of Ungentlemanly Warfare') in Bombay. One of his jobs was to keep an eye on movement control and he was thus able to locate my brother-in-law Bill who was attached to the Royal Maritime Regiment.

When I visited Angus some years ago he gave me a book to read called *The Boarding Party* by James Leasor and I must say it was one of the most enjoyable war books I had ever read. Although Angus hadn't taken an active part in the actual boarding of the ship concerned, his boss had done all the planning and Angus had helped in some measure to put the plan into action, though neither of them were mentioned. Angus's boss was Colonel Colin Hercules MacKenzie, who was responsible for most of the clandestine operations in the South East Asia Command. A film entitled 'The Sea Wolves' was subsequently made of the book but it wasn't half as entertaining as it didn't portray the build-up to the action, particularly with regard to the 'Oldies' who took part in it.

Angus's nickname for me was 'Chrissie Bolshie'. The reason for this is unknown, unless it refers to a Bolshevik. Perhaps it was when he refused to bring me to a dance at Cameron Barracks, where he was stationed for a short time. He said he didn't want his kid sister to mix with 'Swadddies' (not 'Squaddies' as they were called elsewhere) and said I was too much of a 'Bolshie' wanting to mix with the rabble. He must have forgotten that he was once a 'Swaddie' himself but, between the wars, soldiers were looked down upon in the same way as Kipling's 'Tommy':

For it's Tommy this and Tommy that an' "Chuck him out, the brute!"
But it's "Saviour of 'is country" when the guns begin to shoot.

Nevertheless Angus brought me to some of the 'Invitation' dances in the town when I was eighteen and I always enjoyed them.

Kenny was a completely different type from Angus. Even their hair colouring was different, Kenny being almost platinum-haired to Angus's light brown. Kenny was more like my mum's people and Angus more like the Chisholms. Although born and brought up in the barracks, Ken had no leanings towards the military life and he seemed to go through his teenage years singing the latest songs and trying the latest dance steps, which I copied; particularly the 'Charleston' and the 'Black Bottom'. The songs I remember hearing him singing were 'Ramona', 'Because I love you' and 'Ki-ki-ki-Katie'. I was amazed when my son Donald, on his first visit home from college, told me that he had heard a lovely new song called 'Ramona' which he thought I would like and he gave me a record of it. He was surprised to hear that it had been one of my favourite teenage melodies. Again, when my daughter Marion was living in Norway, she sent me a tape of musician friends, with one of the group playing 'Ramona' on the tuba; so it seems the air has universal appeal. Kenny's other main interest was his place in the 'Sheep's Bags' football team, which was the local team. Officially called the 'Citadel Football Team', it was based at Shore Street Park and the colours were red. I think that first of all Ken worked in the railway because I remember we had beautiful brass swans on the kitchen mantelpiece which he had made in the workshops there but, for his lifetime career, he was an electrical engineer. Like the other brothers, Ken was a keen piper and played in the Boys' Brigade Pipe Band but, as a dancer, he was far ahead of the others and once beat the reigning World Champion Highland Dancer. Kenny was never too busy to have a word with or help out any of his younger siblings. When I was seven and fell victim to Scarlet Fever, I cried that I didn't want anyone but Kenny to carry me downstairs to the ambulance – so he did – and he cried too as he was very soft hearted. However, I was soon well again and up to my usual tricks. Ken's nickname for me was 'Tommack', being Invernessian for 'Tomboy'. I couldn't really avoid being a tomboy in those days as my elder sister was eight years older and my younger sister was four years younger. The boys were nearer my age and I was very keen on games and outdoor pursuits, whereas my sisters were always far more ladylike!

During World War II when I was in the services and stationed in London, I loved to visit Ken and his wife Louie in their home in Stowmarket, Suffolk, where Ken was in a reserved occupation working for the Electricity Authority connected with the American air bases in East Anglia. What heaven it was to waken in Stowmarket, after a particularly gruelling time in London, to a beautiful breakfast served up on a dainty tray by Louie. She and Ken were a delightful couple and we christened them 'The Lovebirds' during their courtship days, long, long ago. Ken imbibed a lot of the Highland literature and traditions from my Dad as well as from some of the monks in Beauly Priory and Pluscarden Abbey, Elgin, where he used to work now and then in connection with the electricity supply. He became something of an expert on clan history and disputed statements regarding the Strathglass Chisholms being originally from the Lowlands. He maintained that the Strathglass Chisholms had come through the north of Scotland from Orkney and Norway, not through the Normans to the borders, where there is a place called Chisholm. They were probably from a different branch. Kenny's elder son, Kenneth, was the only grandson of my father to play the bagpipes, so he became the heir to the family heirloom. This was a pipe banner which belonged to one of the Chiefs of the Chisholms of Strathglass, Roderick Donald Matheson Chisholm,

The Chisholm of Chisholm, 28th Chief of the Clan Chisholm, who died in 1887 without issue. Subsequent to this Chief's death, the chiefship went down the female line twice-removed; so Dad, with delusions of grandeur, maintained that he had as much right to the chiefship! I'm afraid that would mean very little as the present Chief owns no land or buildings in Strathglass and there are more Chisholms in Nova Scotia than there are in Strathglass.

To look at, Ian rather resembled my father, being of smaller stature than Ken and he had a slight tinge of sandy gold in his hair like Dad. He was always on the lookout for a laugh and used to enjoy taking the mickey out of any of us who were getting too hoity-toity. He had a motorbike and was rather a daredevil on it. I remember going on it once and it seemed as if we were doing a hundred miles an hour as he went careering round Deveron Street, up George Street, Rose Street and then down Innes Street with me screaming on the pillion and Ian laughing all the way. It was the last time I ever went on his bike and I'd never go on another. Like the others Ian was keen on the bagpipes and Highland dancing but he didn't practise much either and, as often as not, when dancing in a competition, something would happen; his sporran or balmoral would fall off or his pumps would become unlaced. I don't think he cared all that much about his appearance, yet when as a Rover Scout, he and a few other Inverness Rovers were told by the Scout hierarchy that they must not wear balmorals but the official Scout bush hat with their kilted Scout uniforms, they clung to their balmorals and went to their leader, pointing out how incongruous the bush hat looked with the kilt. They won their case and continued to wear the balmoral but, whether or not it was an official victory, I don't know and I haven't seen any Scouts wearing balmorals for years.

I used to enjoy a 'scud' (as we called a ride) in the huge basket Ian had in front of his bike when he worked after school as a 'bowsher', as we called the errand boys who delivered 'messages' (groceries etc.). He couldn't, even if he wanted to, do 100 mph on that bike!

Ian had also been born and brought up at Cameron Barracks. Although he trained as an electrical engineer, he had a lifelong desire to join the Army and military heroes were his heroes. He got as far as joining the Territorial Army in peacetime and was called up in 1939 but, after serving with the 51st (Highland) Division and the 52nd (Lowland) Division under his hero General Montgomery, he was transferred to the Royal Engineers, winning the Belgian *Croix de Guerre* with Palm. However after the war Ian told me he had changed his mind about the Army being a good career and said he was quite glad to return to civilian life, particularly as he still retained some shrapnel from wounds he had received. He had to have regular trips to Edenhall Hospital in Edinburgh to have pieces of shrapnel removed periodically. Ian never spoke about his medal awards but I remember, when I was on leave once during the war, my mother receiving a letter from a twelve-year old Dutch boy who had written to her (I don't know how he got her address) praising Ian and saying that he (the Dutch boy) was going to write to Mr Churchill about help Ian had given to his family and the people of his town or village. We heard no more about this and Ian never spoke about his experiences and besides the medal was a Belgian award, not a Dutch one, so it remains a mystery.

Ian was very popular with girls and I know I was often invited to parties by girls so that I would bring Ian as a partner. If he wasn't top notch in the piping and dancing scales, he was in the singing. No-one could sing 'Lochnagar' or 'O Hi-ri-ri tha e tighinn' ('Hip-hip hooray, he is coming' – 'he' being Bonnie Prince Charlie) like Ian and he had a repertoire of Jacobite and Gaelic songs which he was always singing. Other favourite songs were 'The Big Rock-Candy Mountain' and 'Cigarettes and Whisky and Wild, Wild Women' and he had learnt a lot of 'Rebel' songs and 'King Billy' songs from some of the Glasgow/Irish boys he had met during his term with the Royal Engineers.

Ian could take a tune out of anything: a ruler on a desk, a line of glass tumblers, a Jew's Harp or even a pencil by striking it against his own teeth. He had annoying habits though; often, when sitting down reading a newspaper near Ian, he would suddenly put his hand under the paper and shoot it sky-high above my head, much to his amusement but not to mine.

Had Callum kept a professional interest in piping, no doubt he would have been one of the foremost exponents of his day, but he loved the pipes and pipe music for their own sake and the pleasure it gave him and his listeners. He was an expert on the history of the Highland bagpipe and the *piobaireachd*. I found it fascinating to hear the story behind such famous 'Pibrochs' as 'The Lament for the Children', being a lament by one of the famous MacCrimmons of Skye for the death of seven of his sons. They had died around the same time as a result of smallpox, brought ashore by a seaman who had landed at Dunvegan and spread the disease. Then 'The Battle of the Birds' was just as fascinating as one can almost hear the screeches as they dashed each other to pieces. I would complain that it was a waste of syrup when I saw my Dad and brothers heating up the syrup tin and pouring it into the bag of the bagpipes; but it was explained to me that it wasn't a waste and was necessary to keep the bag in trim and, in any case, I never had to do without syrup on my porridge (I preferred syrup to milk on my porridge). Callum was exceptionally tall for his age and became a six-footer but I think my mother thought that, as he was thin, he was a trifle delicate and I used to be miffed when he had eggs for breakfast and I had the usual plate of porridge. Of course it was pure jealousy on my part for I really enjoyed my morning plate of porridge and I still like it but have to watch the calories. I used to go round the table looking for the lumpiest plate of porridge and even stole the raw oatmeal out of the larder, until Dad stopped that by telling me I'd get worms.

Callum used to devour all the latest comics, which resulted in his having occasional nightmares, when he would get out of bed and dance around the room like a ballet dancer. We called Callum 'Skinny-ma-Linky Longlegs' but Angus called him 'Gallaleepi-Snipe'. I don't know if this was perhaps a corruption of 'Gallipoli Sniper' and I never found out. Angus composed a pipe tune which he called 'Gallaleepie Dances in the Firelight', as we had fires in our bedrooms and when Callum was dancing, he threw shadows on the walls.

Callum and his friend Cecil used to raid gardens where there were apple trees but, of course, our parents knew nothing about this. Incidentally we didn't pronounce Cecil's name as most do. His family and everyone else called him 'See-sawl'. Callum and Cecil's most daring raid was to the Headmaster's garden and, as the Headmaster lived on the hill district, quite far from our house, this was just a piece of bravado. We had a youngish neighbour who used to play host to all the youngsters round about, probably because her husband was a tradesman who had to be away a lot working in the islands. She was left with her two young children and probably found the evenings long. She helped us girls to cut out dress patterns and we used to make quite fashionable silk or satin underwear and would even venture as far as making summer dresses and evening gowns.

When we were going to a special dance, we used to buy a face pack and Nellie, this kind lady, helped us to apply it. However, one night the boys brought their hoard of apples into her house and Nellie was not pleased with them, pointing out that, although they thought it great fun and a great achievement, they were really stealing, when it came to the bit. Callum was the ringleader and, just as Nellie was wondering what to do with the 'loot', my mother's head appeared round the door and Nellie just had time to throw a cushion on the chair on top of the apples and sit on it. She said afterwards that she had never sat on such a hot seat, terrified that my mum would discover the apples. The boys must have taken her advice seriously as I never remember their stealing apples after that. Anyway, they were usually cookers and I didn't enjoy eating them, despite them being forbidden fruit.

Being in a reserved occupation as a telegraph installer in the railway, Callum wasn't allowed to join the services during the war but was posted to Glasgow, a more strategic area, as far as his work was concerned. He used to call me 'Jonah' as he said I was always around when anything calamitous happened. This was borne out early in the war when I went down to Glasgow for the weekend and, just as we were going home to a cousin's house with Callum and my cousin's boyfriend, there was a 'whoosh' and down came a bomb. This was the first air-raid I had experienced and I think it was one of the first raids on Glasgow. I don't think it was all that bad and nothing like the London raids I experienced later but my cousin lived in a tenement in Partick, which fairly shook when the Merkland Subway was hit. I believe a bomb dropped down the funnel of a ship called, I think, *HMS Suffolk* which was in the docks.

After the war, Callum emigrated to America to help my brother Jack set up the Washington Pipe Band and, although he had quite a good job there with the Atomic Energy Authority there, he preferred the Highland way of life and returned to Inverness after a couple of years.

Alex, whose correct name was Alexander John Cameron Chisholm, was called after two nephews of my father who had both been killed in the First World War. Alex played the pipes and performed Highland dancing but his love was singing and he was forever regaling us with sentimental ballads, such as 'Helen of Kirkconnel Lea', 'Jock o' Hazeldean' or Gaelic songs and when he went to the Forces, his *forté* was 'A bunch of Violets' (about a girl jilting her soldier lover for a rich man) and 'Army Jam'. He used to sing his favourite songs to his children and my children loved to hear his singing of 'Army Jam':

> *Army jam, Army jam, we all love Army jam;*
> *Plum, apple, apricot, sent from Dundee in tin pots*
> *And, every night when I'm asleep, I'm dreaming that I am*
> *Bombing old Fritz, blowing him to bits …*
> *With a tin of ARMY JAM …*

Alex was a Scout and often used to sing at their concerts. He had lots of friends of his own age nearby and there was always some scheme afloat among them. He often won prizes for singing Gaelic and, even after his voice broke, there remained a sweetness of expression which remained as he became older and he always led the sing-songs at family reunions and weddings. Like Ian, Alex became a 'bowsher' after school and some of his pals did likewise. Sometimes when they met *en route* with their deliveries, they would exchange notes and would swap 'messages' that would take them out of their usual route, if they fell in with someone who was going in that particular direction. They often went camping together at the weekends in a field near Culloden House during the summer months and there would be no shortage of food as the grocery 'bowsher' would bring groceries, the butcher's 'bowsher' would bring butcher meat and so on. They had it all worked out to a fine art.

Alex broke the usual routine of the male members of the family in that he took a Commercial course at school and started his career as a clerk and, eventually became an assessor with the local authority in Inverness and, after the war, with Lothian Region. After Munich in 1938, Alex joined the Territorial Army Cameron Highlanders and was sent to France at the outbreak of War in September 1939, where he worked at Battalion headquarters with the 51st (Highland) Division. In June 1940, between Alex's 18th and 19th birthdays the Belgians capitulated, the French turned tail and ran and the Germans demolished the supposedly impregnable Maginot Line. The Fifty-First was thus caught in a trap at St Valery en Caux in France and Alex was wounded at the beginning of the bombardment on 6th June. Although the Highlanders put up a good defence, it was an impossible situation as they were cut off from Dunkirk and encircled by the Germans and, when all else failed, General Fortune was forced to surrender. The TA Camerons of those days was composed of men from the town and county of Inverness (including Skye and the Inverness-shire islands) and most of the men knew each other in civvy street or at the annual TA camp. When Alex was wounded two of the older men who had lived near us carried him into a wood and hid him there just before the Germans arrived and took the division into captivity for the rest of the war, most of them being sent to Silesian prisoner-of-war camps. Alex told me afterwards that he seemed to have lain there for days and that, when two French soldiers came along and he asked them for a drink, they refused unless he could give them cigarettes – so much for the vaunted 'Auld Alliance'! However, he was eventually found by the Red Cross and was fortunate enough to be back in 'Blighty' within the next couple of days.

At that time in 1940 the Highland newspapers were full of banner headlines, because there didn't seem to be the smallest hamlet from Lochaber to Badenoch and the Outer Hebrides to Orkney and Shetland that hadn't someone serving in the Fifty-First in France. There were long pages of local newspapers full of photographs of Highland boys marked 'Missing, believed Killed' or 'Captured'. Fortunately for my parents, before the lists were published with Alex's photo captioned

'Missing', they got a letter from Alex saying he was in Bangour Hospital, Bathgate, wounded but getting on fine. Next day, the usual War Office telegram arrived to say he was missing! It goes to show the chaos which was caused by the breakthrough on the Maginot line and the ineptitude of the French Command, which led to the evacuation at Dunkirk and the capture of the famous 'Fifty-First'.

When I visited Alex at Bangour shortly afterwards and he came to meet me, I nearly fainted, as one of his sleeves was hanging empty and I thought the worst. It turned out that the nerves in his left arm were shattered and his arms full of bullet wounds and shrapnel. However, with careful nursing and the use of a contraption made up of individual fingerstalls attached to a ring of elastic at his wrist, he was able to regain a certain amount of use of his hand through time. It was just as well that he was a sedentary worker and not a tradesman and that his right hand was unaffected. He was subsequently discharged from the Army on medical grounds but was given a silver badge to wear on his civvies so that people would know he had served in the forces and there would be no reason to give him a white feather, as was the habit sometimes.

If there was a holy terror in our family, it was Jack or Jackie (correct name John). He was the one who saw all sorts of mischievous possibilities in any situation and he was the only one, as far as I remember, who was the cause of a policeman calling at the house. This was for throwing a lighted firework into the doorstep of one of the crusty old maids who lived in the street. It's not that he intended to hurt anyone (he said) but he resented some of the things she did, such as the way she kept any ball that went into her wee garden, instead of returning it when he rang the bell politely and asked for it. Of course, Jack was made to see the error of his ways in meting out his rough justice and he continued to get into trouble at home, but not with the police. When he was angry about anything, he would concentrate all his venom into his nearly black eyes and his forehead and beetling brows would furrow, as when he called another grumpy woman a 'Dame' and her husband told him he must never again call his wife that, the word being used in Inverness in a derogatory sense for an annoying woman.

One always spoke of Alex and Jack together and there were only eighteen months between them. They went about a lot together, Alex's easy-going nature being a foil for Jack's high spirits. They joined the TA together. Jack was in the pipe band and I used to be almost in tears when I saw him on parade. I said to my mother, "I saw the Fourth Cameron's Band today and poor Jackie looks so wee there besides the others". Indeed, when time came for the Regiment to go overseas and Alex went, Jack was considered too young so he was kept in the north of Scotland training centre and then transferred to an English regiment. I can't remember if it was the Green Howards or the Sherwood Foresters but he had a huge green diamond cloth patch which practically covered the back of his khaki uniform. (Who says the kilt is odd military wear when one remembers Jack's outfit?). Jack was eventually attached to the Royal Artillery and spent most of his war years in Greece and the Mediterranean.

Jack had initially trained as a laboratory assistant in an Inverness hospital and used to bring home some trophies from his work, one being a guinea pig which used to follow Mum around the house. The other side of his nature often came to the fore and he brought home a jar one day with horrible looking contents which he blithely informed us were "Mrs S--'s guts". This Mrs S --- was one of the infamous street characters in the town and she had been knocked down and killed by a car and no doubt a post-mortem had been arranged. I was almost sick to hear this and still shiver at the memory of the contents of the jar; but it now occurs to me that it could just have been one of Jack's tricks. When he got tired of shocking us, he decided to train as a motor mechanic and I think he worked on the mechanical side in the Army. After being demobilised he joined the Edinburgh City Police (he had grown tall despite my misgivings at the beginning of the war) and he worked mostly on the transport side. Sometimes he used to run-in a car by taking a jaunt up to Inverness. Besides, at that time, the City of Edinburgh Police had the most famous pipe band in the world and a lot of Jack's police service was spent travelling with the band, even to South Africa on one occasion. Except perhaps Angus who had undergone a Pipe Major's course at Edinburgh Castle and had been a Pipe-Major in peacetime before being commissioned, of all the brothers I think Jackie was the most skilled piper. He loved the pipes so much that he left the police and emigrated to Washington, USA, where he was asked to form and teach a pipe band, at the same time being able to pursue his trade in the motor industry there. He arranged to have the band dressed in Chisholm tartan. Jack and Callum were invited to play at President John Kennedy's inauguration ceremony. They had photographs of this event with the President standing with them and an autographed inscription to that effect.

Jack was a wizard with the artist's brush and was also skilled at drawing. He used to write ditties about school when he was young and his most famous one was "Tis Treachery, 'Tis True', being a condemnation of having to go to school when the weather was fine and more suitable for outdoor pursuits.

As a child, Paddy was the most adorable looking little boy, with the unusual combination of dark brown eyes and very fair, curly hair. When Paddy grew older he hated his curly hair and used to spend hours in front of the mirror almost in tears, trying to smooth it down with water, which I suppose only encouraged the hair to curl.

By the time Paddy arrived in the family, we were all ready to adore him anyway and, although he was spoilt quite a lot, being the youngest, he withstood the effect and grew up a strong character in his own right. He was a leader from the very beginning and, in the family, we used to call him, 'King of the Kids' as the other children of the neighbourhood looked up to him as leader. Of course, as well as being petted, the brothers used to tease him a lot and this was expected in a large family. His companion in childhood was Marie, my younger sister and they were always spoken of together.

I think at first Paddy was a Cub Scout as I remember one Scout concert where he was dressed in a crepe paper crinoline and poke bonnet dancing the Petronella with some other Cubs; but I also remember his being in The Boys' Brigade. I think it must have been quite common for boys to change their allegiance from Scouts to BB as the spirit moved them but, in the case of my brothers it always seemed to be the company with the best pipe band.

We wondered at his being named Paddy when he wasn't an Irishman and we had no Irish connections but Dad said he had wanted his name registered as *Padruig*, the Gaelic for Patrick or Peter, a family name. However the Registrar couldn't enter a Gaelic name and wanted an English equivalent. The authorities relented in about 1973, and as Registrar of Births, etc. for North Skye, I got a letter informing me that Gaelic names could now be registered, provided an English translation was included after the name. I cannot understand why the native Gaels put up with such discrimination. My mum told me that the abominable second name Jessie was given to me in similar circumstances. I used to say it sounded like a horse and hated it and would never tell anyone what the 'J' in my initials stood for. I am called after my mother's mum (Christina) and Mum's granny (*Seonaid*) but, as *Seonaid* was barred by the Inverness Registrar, Dad forgot the literal translation of Janet and opted for Jessie as an alternative.

In Paddy's case, it was only at school he was called Patrick and he didn't mind being called Paddy. To annoy him, some of the brothers would call him 'Peechter the Teuchter' or 'Peter the Hermit' and sometimes he would be subjected to the chant:

> *Paddy was an Irishman, Paddy was a thief.*
> *Paddy came to my house and stole a leg of beef.*
> *I went to Paddy's house but Paddy wasn't in –*
> *So I took a red-hot poker and hit him on the chin.*

What nonsense that makes, but I once heard an English girl quoting a similar rhyme about 'Taffy was a Welshman ...', so it's probably one of those old children's rhyming games.

Although the whole of our family was steeped in stories and tales of 'The Regiment' and my parents still corresponded with ex-Cameron comrades, Paddy was an exception in that he joined the Royal Navy when his time came to enlist during the war. He spoke of a most interesting time travelling all round the world and he and I were reminiscing once about the time we met in London and visited the widow of Mum's uncle Kenneth (the only one who could out-talk Dad and had travelled the world). We called her 'Auntie Rosa' and she was a real Cockney who insisted on bringing us round to her 'local' later on in the night, where we all ended up in a circle with hands on shoulders, kicking our knees up like high-steppers while everyone sang, 'Knees up, Mother Brown ...' with the sound of exploding bombs outside. Aunt Rosa was a tiny wee thing but had the typical Cockney sense of humour which I came to admire during the war years. Her husband had referred to her as 'the threepenny bit' when talking about her as she was so small and he was over six feet tall. Rosa lived in Camberwell and, even after being bombed out on several occasions she refused to leave London. She brought me to Camberwell Cemetery to see Great Uncle Kenneth's grave, which was very near the grave of John Ruskin.

Paddy had a canary as a pet and, if he was in one of those moods, when he thought no-one loved him, or when he got into hot water over something, he would say, "All right then, I'm going away to the hills", and Mum would say, "Well, if that's what you want, just go". Then Paddy would say, "But I want my bird", whereupon the cage would be handed to him and he would go to the door but, ten minutes afterwards, he would reappear with the cage in a complete change of mood and the episode would be forgotten – until the next time.

Although Dad started to teach Paddy the pipes and the older brothers tried to help, Paddy decided he would rather learn to play the violin and went for lessons to Sara Walker's School of Music in Academy Street in Inverness. He did quite well but had to take a lot of ragging from his brothers, particularly from Ian, who said one day, "You know, Paddy, you play like Paderewski". Paddy replied scathingly, "Paderewski couldn't play the fiddle". Ian's reply was, "Well, neither can you!" However, once he grew up, Paddy forsook the fiddle for the bagpipes and became hooked on them like his brothers. Paddy never really outgrew his crown as 'King of the Kids' as, over the years, he encouraged and accompanied his children to their various activities – swimming, sports, etc. and enjoyed partaking of them himself. The brothers were football buffs and Paddy played for local football team Clachnacuddin.

Which girl could grow up conceited or with a superiority complex with seven brothers who would make such remarks as, "If your face was your fortune, you'd die in the poorhouse", or "If you were hanged for being good-looking, you would die innocent." (This when I'd be titivating before going to a dance). Another gibe, when trying to scrounge something from me would be, "If you were a ghost you wouldn't give me a fright", or, "If you owned the Sahara Desert, you wouldn't give me a grain of sand". Callum was a great admirer of Disraeli and when he thought I used too big a word, he would say, "You are intoxicated (I think Disraeli said 'Inebriated') with the exuberance of your own verbosity", or "You are havering under a multitude of disarranged ideas". His favourite quiz was asking us younger ones, "D'you know what this means? 'A slight inclination of the cranium is equivalent to a spasmodic movement of the optic as far as an equine quadruped devoid of its visionary capacity is concerned.'" Of course we had no answer to this and it was years before we knew what was meant. The younger brothers had a secret language which was quite easily decipherable, although they thought it was very clever; but it was quite easy to know what was meant by "Ificky I-icky hadicky myicky money-icky withicky me-icky, I-icky wouldicky buy-icky thaticky thingicky". Another trick was, when speaking about girls, to spell the girls' names backwards to try to fool us but we knew at once that the name 'Tebro Cattie' meant Etta Corbett who lived down the Longman and was one of Alex's girlfriends.

On the other hand, the brothers could be very kind to me. I remember Angus sending me a beautiful three-foot necklace of real ivory and a string of black pearls from India and Ian gave me my first wrist watch which he bought on his first TA camp at Barry. Kenny was always generous and gave us many treats but Callum and the rest of us depended on our elders for treats and were quite penniless until we started work ourselves.

My brothers would combine in playing tricks. When I was little and my parents were both in church on Sunday evenings and they were left in charge, one of their horrible stunts was to lie me on a bed, remove my shoes and socks and start tickling the soles of my feet with a feather. How I laughed but it was a laugh of pure agony, if that were possible. It certainly wasn't pleasurable. Another bad thing (or good thing, according to how one looks at it) was that they instilled into me a dread of experiencing an electric shock. The cause of all this was Ken and Ian's habit of wiring all the brass bedroom door-knobs to batteries. When I put my hand on the knob, I'd get a terrible electric shock. I remember once I accompanied my elder brothers to some friend's aunt's house in Nairn. There was a peacock on the lawn and we were thrilled to see the wonderful bird; but I only remember that day vividly because the brothers made us all stand holding hands in a line on the lawn while, at one end one of them had an electric wire plugged into a battery and the other fellow at the other end did likewise. At first it wasn't too bad but, when they increased the voltage, we couldn't tear our hands away from each other and I started screaming until they had to release me. I still get a start today if electrical appliances blow a fuse.

Nevertheless, the brothers used to encourage my keenness on hockey and tennis and were quite proud when I was made Vice-Captain of the school hockey team. I didn't consider myself to be a great player but I was always picked for the first eleven and, on Saturdays, we were often away at Dingwall, Fortrose, Nairn or Elgin playing another school team. We used to wear cashmere or woollen double-kneed black stockings to school in those days, although sometimes we wore royal-blue stockings to match our gym girdles for hockey. Anyway, I wasn't in the least put out when my mother complained that that was the second pair of stocking knees I had torn during the fortnight. I wondered why she should be so upset about it and said, "Och, Mammy, it's all in the game!" It never occurred to me that clothing ten children was an expensive business. However, on the odd Saturday mornings when I wasn't playing hockey I used to offer to make the scones and my mum seemed quite glad of the offer. My scones weren't a patch on my mum's but no doubt it gave her a little time away from the cooker.

The brothers were very good at seeing that us sisters got a good share of any of the games we were playing and also at seeing us through the long, dark, front lobby before dashing upstairs at night. They were a protection against any neighbourhood bully ... but I don't remember ever being bullied by the boys in the street, as they were nearly all friendly with at least one of my brothers. When I became a teenager, my friend Rene and I became 'pals' with David and Barty – two of the boys in the street – and we went around together after school.

Before Angus went to India we had a family group taken at a local photographer's studio and we were all in Highland dress. Some newspaperman must have seen it in the showcase they used to have in the studio window and it appeared in print with the caption, 'A Real Highland Family' detailing all our names and saying that we were all pipers and dancers. We were all very embarrassed but we were already quite well known in the town and it was a good likeness with yours truly, according to the boys, "Posing like a fish-supper on a cold morning" (whatever that means!). There is a Gaelic song which laments the dispersal of the Highlanders and, when I look at that photo today and remember how we all left home and scattered, I can see what the composer meant when one remembers all the generations who emigrated from the Highlands.

When the radio first appeared, Ken and Ian built one and I used to love, during my homework session, to listen to music on it. The boys used to experiment and one night decided to play a joke on Dad. They caused an announcement to be made (by themselves in the next room) to the effect that some famous piper was to give a recital on the wireless at such and such a time and my father made arrangements to switch on at the given time. When the piping recital started, there was no name given and Dad was trying to guess who was playing as he knew all the best pipers of his day. At last he said, "Whoever that is, he's not very expert – our Ian could play better than that". Poor Ian, although a good piper, he didn't win as many prizes as the rest and had the name of not trying hard enough. Little did Dad know until later that it WAS Ian who was playing! Once the boys got into hot water when Dad had one of his friends visiting and they put over an SOS, asking Murdo to report home at once. Poor Murdo had been sitting in a chair close to the wireless and I remember seeing him jumping up and overturning his chair in confusion with his face turned ashen. Ken and Ian really got a good telling-off for that mischief. Another time I remember was that my Dad had set aside a cod he was going to give a neighbour from his fishing trip on the Moray Firth with Murdo, who was co-owner of their wee boat. Dad had put the fish on the sink for wrapping up, when Kenny came in with a fresh loaf from Anderson's the baker in Academy Street at the foot of Rose Street. The loaf was just out of the oven and, coming home, Kenny had succumbed to the temptation of taking bits out with his fingers to eat on the way home. When he got home he noticed there was quite a hole in the loaf and he didn't want to get a row so, quick-witted as usual, he decided he would stuff the head of the fish into the hole in the loaf and say that the fish must have eaten it. All was forgiven when Mum and Dad came across the 'bread-eating' fish as it gave them a good laugh.

The boys always bought comics. I remember Kenny's favourites were Harold Lloyd in 'Film Fun' and 'Cardew the Cad'. The younger boys read 'The Dandy', 'The Beano', 'The Hotspur' and 'The Adventure' and 'Oor Wullie' and 'The Broons' in the *Sunday Post*. We used to get American comics from friends with 'The Katzenjammer Kids', 'Little Orphan Annie', 'Mutt and Jeff' and 'Maggie & Jiggs'. Jiggs loved corned beef and cabbage and, when we had corned-beef hash that was called 'Jigg's Dinner'. I can't remember if it was the Scottish newspaper called the *Bulletin* which also featured 'Maggie & Jiggs' but it gave great hilarity to our parents and their neighbours – especially Jiggs's Lowrie-like matchstick dog Fido. However, when the *Daily Record* was taken over by the Mirror Group of newspapers, my parents stopped buying it and they bought instead the *Daily Mail* (or *Express*, I'm not sure which) and 'Flook' took over from Fido as their favourite cartoon character.

Alex and Jack slept in the same bed and Paddy slept in a single bed in the same room and, after official 'Lights Out', they would read out the jokes to Paddy, asking him some riddles, etc. In fact, whenever Jack told a joke, he told it as if he were reading it, saying the words in parenthesis, as in the written word. We couldn't help laughing at some of their quizzes, for instance, "What is the height of impossibility?" Answer: "An elephant hanging over a cliff with his tail tied to a daisy". Another favourite was, "If it takes a man a week to walk a fortnight, how long will it take a fly with a pair of navvy's boots on to walk over a barrel of tar?" Answer: "As long as it will take to sandpaper an elephant down to a greyhound".

Looking back, I think I had a very secure, enjoyable childhood as a member of a large family, where I think most of us got the corners rubbed off and yet managed to hold our own, each as an individual character with different tastes and hobbies.

We didn't have television or the sophisticated equipment children have today, but I don't think today's children have as much FUN as we had. We had to rely so much on improvisation that we became quite creative and we were all children of the great outdoors. In the holidays (if we weren't going away with our parents) we went with friends to Bunchrew or Culloden to gather blaeberries and raspberries and brambles for our mothers' jams and pies. When we were older, we thought nothing of climbing Craig Dunain, Craig Phadraig and Torvean or of a seventeen-mile bike run to Urquhart Castle or to Beauly or Nairn; but of course the roads were quieter in those days. When the Children's Hearing Panel system came into being, I felt I would like to help some of the children who came in front of the panel and served from its inception until I retired. However I found that a lot of today's 'Problem Children' were suffering from the effects of having 'Problem Parents'!

I don't know if it had any significance but, in those days, I think everyone had a church connection, whether Catholic, Protestant, Methodist or Jehovah's Witness, and we all got along well together. On a Sunday evening in Inverness the main streets would be crowded with young people going to church to the sound of the church bells. When I go through to Inverness now, all you hear is the sound of the traffic and the tills in the shops drowning out the bells on a Sunday on our way to church.

CHAPTER 5

'There is no Friend like a Sister in Calm and Stormy Weather'

(Christina Rossetti)

I THOUGHT my elder sister Marion was a wonderful person. She came second in the family, being just about a year younger than Angus and she acted as a deputy mother to us when Mum wasn't around or was busy otherwise. When we came home from school, Marion was usually there first, stationed at the kitchen table, breadknife in hand (no sliced bread then), asking each of us as we came in, "Brown or white, straight or curled, butter or jam, double or single?" We then went happily outside with our choice of pieces but for some unknown reason, I was the only member of the household who didn't like butter *and* jam on bread – just jam or butter. We would stay outside playing until Dad came in at around five o'clock for his tea. The railway offices were quite near Innes Street and Dad always came home at midday for his dinner as we all did in those days, there being no such thing as school dinners. When we went to secondary school 'Up the hill', it was one mad rush, down Stephen's Brae, through the back station to Strothers Lane and Railway Terrace and then down Innes Street to eat our dinner and then hurry all the way back to school.

As well as being good-natured, Marion was extremely good-looking, with dark brown eyes and jet black hair and, when she told me that she intended marrying the then Prince of Wales (afterwards King Edward VIII and Duke of Windsor), I was not at all surprised and thought he would get the better bargain. I thought that, as she managed to control us lot, she would be well able to manage him too. We had seen him on a visit to Inverness and the north and I thought they would be a good match, in my ignorance, not realising how impossible it would be for Marion to meet him on a social footing. When Marina, Princess of Greece, married the then Duke of Kent, we all saw a striking resemblance to Marion but, by that time, Marion was walking out with her best love, William (Bill) MacKenzie, whom she eventually married. They made a handsome pair and with Marion's best friend Alice and Bill's pal, Willie Matheson, they went everywhere together with Alice and Marion usually dressed alike and the boys in grey flannels and blazers. We used to call them, 'MacKenzie Bill and Matheson Will'. Sadly, 'Matheson Will' was serving with the Air Force when Singapore fell to the Japanese during the war and we never heard what became of him.

The neighbours used to look up to Marion as a leader of fashion, although she was always quietly dressed, and they would come to the house with hats, etc. for Marion's approval or otherwise. One neighbour's husband was very superstitious and wouldn't allow anything green in his house and when his wife Maggie took a fancy to a green hat, she had to hide it at first and then brought it to Marion, who liked it very much. Maggie begged Marion to bring the hat to her house and "Get round Jock", as she said, by telling him that it suited Maggie so well in would be a shame to return it to the shop … and Maggie won her point and kept the hat. This Jock was a painter and decorator to trade and was very keen on portrait painting. He liked to paint on glass and did one of me in my bridesmaid's dress at Marion's wedding, complete with tinsel tiara. The portrait was beautifully done, as far as the clothing was concerned but the face bore no resemblance. He did another of my father in full Highland dress, which was really outstanding as far as the detail was concerned but the face wasn't really like Dad and the eyes were staring – so much so that, shortly before Dad died, in his own room at home where the picture hung, his mind started wandering and he asked my mother who was that awful man who kept staring at him.

As far as I remember, I never had flowers sent to me by an admirer but my admirers were very few. Marion often had bouquets or corsages sent to the house by some admirer who had asked her to a ball. The brothers called one such 'Tulips' as he always sent those flowers to her. Although he was a fairly well-off young business man, she wasn't all that impressed by him but always enjoyed going to dances and balls. She was an expert Highland dancer and, when my father was asked to bring dancers to perform at some special event, Marion was always included. In fact they were asked to dance before the late ex-King Alfonso of Spain at Castle Leod near Strathpeffer but Marion just acted as coolly as if it were a concert in aid of the orphanage or some other charity. I would have fainted with fright!

Marion was an excellent cook and housewife and seemed to like housework, which I didn't. When time came for tidying up, somehow or other (and unintentionally, I honestly assure you) I always seemed to have something or other more pressing to do and would say, "I'm just going to", when asked if I had dried the dishes. Another of my family nicknames became "Just going to" and a friend worked a pun on that in a poem she composed called 'Jess going to' (being my hated middle name Jessie). It went something like this:

What would the happy family do, without their own 'Jess going to'?
Poor mother tries to keep her right and father also joins the fight,
"Have you done what I told you to?" "Yes, Father, I'm Jess going to".

I don't think I did much housework or cooking and my free time seemed to be taken up with music, hockey or play. Sometimes when I'd really try to help, Marion would say, "Oh, leave it, that's not the right way to do it – I'll do it myself." I must admit I was always a bit of a dreamer and used to break dishes and drop things and this led to another nickname, 'Calamity Kate' (not 'Calamity Jane'). It's surprising that, when I married at twenty-three, I wasn't very experienced or competent as a housekeeper but, by then I was serving in the women's forces with orderlies to do the housework and cooking.

Marion and Marie, my younger sister, shared a bedroom with me and at weekends when having a long lie, Marion would produce her weekly box of chocolates (given by her boy-friend) and Marie and I would curl up in our bed for a feed. I remember that, in order to spread the treat out longer, we used the curly end of a safety pin to scoop out the raspberry creams, in the same way as we used to scoop out the winkles we gathered at the Longman.

One never saw children out in our street playing on a Sunday, as it just wasn't done and Sunday was considered a day of rest. Even yet, I'm all for Sunday being a time off from the everyday chores and stress of life, not just on religious grounds. When in Germany, in a city of about a quarter of a million inhabitants, we were told by the owners of our hotel that we need not expect to be served in German shops or restaurants on a Sunday, as Sunday was considered a family day by them and the only places open would be those premises owned by Greeks or Italians. This at a time when this particular city was celebrating its founding by Caesar Augustus two thousand years previously and it was packed to overflowing with visitors from all over the world – and yet they wanted to keep their Sunday tradition alive.

We went to church and Sunday school and when we were younger, went for walks with my father who usually brought his silver mounted walking stick with the Cameron crest to point out all the interesting things *en route*.

Sometimes, when the weather wasn't good, we would all gather in our kitchen and sing psalms and hymns and our mother would ask us questions from the Catechism. Some of the neighbouring children would join us round the range, and Marion would then produce empty sweetie bags of white paper – the opaque kind and not the modern plastic bags. Although she kept some sweets for Sundays, the bags used during the week were kept so that she would have enough to go round on a Sunday, when we were all given one each and took turns of blowing them up at the corners and handing them back to Marion who would place them upsides-down at the side of the range where they would catch the draught and then she would ask the person who owned that particular bag to wish a wish. She would then light each corner of the bag and, if it went up the chimney, Marion said the wish was granted but, if it just burned where it was, the wish had to be told. Some of the wishes were the usual childish wishes of children of twelve and under but my brother Paddy's wish is often quoted to him. It was a wish 'to live to a ripe old age'. I think mine must have changed pretty often, as I cannot remember wishing for anything in particular, unless it was to achieve my ambitions at that time – to be an author or a concert pianist. Marion was an office worker in Inverness and I remember her once organising a concert party for her firm and I was roped in to appear in the chorus line. What fun we had kicking up our legs like the Bluebell Girls to the tune of 'I want to be Happy'. Later on, during the war when I was at Cameron Barracks, I was asked to organise a chorus and I chose the same format for the opening number. Some years ago, when Marion and I paid a visit to the Moulin Rouge in Paris, we had a laugh about our days in the chorus and thought how different it looked with the beauties on the stage there, with their marvellous figures and long legs.

Marion's husband, Bill, was a very versatile musician and could take a tune out of anything, but his favourite instrument at that time was the accordion. He and some friends started an Accordion Club and used to play at various functions. My childhood friend Ruth and I were given a pair of Indian Clubs each, with a red and green light in each and Bill taught us to swing them to the music in time to the 'Donewellen Waltz' and we really thought we were a great act, when the lights in the hall were put out and our coloured lights encircled the hall. It's not surprising that, for a short time, we were keen to become actresses but I soon lost this ambition when I looked more often in the mirror and decided that the boys were correct when they said that my face wasn't my fortune. We thought, in our ignorance, that only good-looking girls could become actresses. Ruth always wore her hair in a straight bob and I called her 'Japanese Dolly' because I thought she resembled a Japanese doll I had seen in my granny's house in Lewis – probably brought over from Canada when my Aunt Lena was widowed and returned to Lewis with her daughter, cousin Nina.

When I first caught sight of Marie, my younger sister, I thought she was the cutest wee 'living doll' I'd ever seen and as a toddler she was very cuddly with her fair curly hair and blue eyes. Talking of eyes; when she was about three years old, she had a constant habit of sitting on the stair steps with her hands crossed in her lap and she would roll her eyes round and round from stair to ceiling. I used to be quite troubled about this as I was afraid she would spoil her eyes and perhaps become cross-eyed, but she outgrew the habit once she went to school. My mum used to knit beautiful dresses for Marie and her summer dresses always showed off her colouring to the best advantage.

Marie was a natural dancer, with an easy gait and a graceful carriage, whereas the boys told me I had 'an athletic step and feet like ferryboats'. When only seven years of age, Marie won the trophy for dancing at the Northern Musical Festival in Inverness, beating several well-known dancers double her age. She continued her interest in Highland dancing after she grew up and helped Marion with her classes, eventually taking over when Marion and Bill went to live in the country.

Marie and Paddy, being quite close in years, were great companions. I was too old for her when she was younger although, later on, as teenagers, we did sometimes go around together. She had a sweet voice and she and Paddy would often entertain us with duets. 'Clementine' was a special favourite and one of my mother's friends, as a result of this, always called Marie 'Herring Boxes' from the line, 'Herring boxes without topses, sandals were for Clementine'.

What I remember about Marie's wee friends was that they all seemed to do a lot of giggling together. I remember once asking Jackie how old some girl was and he said, "I'm not sure but she will be about Marie's age, as she is a giggly girl like Marie". When I was older and working I remember arranging a summer job in my office for her and her friend to do duplicating work on the Gestetner, addressing envelopes, etc and my colleagues and I used to get a lot of fun listening to their bright chatter.

Marie had several boyfriends when she was a teenager and I was astounded when she told me once that she really liked a certain boy but that nothing would induce her to marry him, as he had red hair.

I could not understand why anyone could be put off a handsome and charming fellow just because of the colour of his hair. We used to say to each other, when we were older, that we hated the idea of living with the same person for a lifetime and that we would rather marry a sailor, who would spend most of his time at sea; or, we said, girls should be allowed to change husbands every seven years. In the event Marie and her husband Will marked many happy wedding anniversaries and my late husband and I celebrated almost forty years of marriage.

Marie worked in the local County Library and during the war, when the male staff were called up, she drove the mobile library van round the country districts of Inverness. However, as war progressed and single women were called up, she spent the rest of the war as a civilian in a precision factory in Glasgow. By this time Marion was married with a child and her husband was serving in the Forces, so she came to live with my parents for the duration.

As far as I remember, Marie wasn't interested in hockey but I remember we used to go together with friends to play tennis after work and in the winter we played badminton. When a teenager, Marie used to go around in a dreamlike state singing, 'Beautiful Dreamer' with a faraway look in her eyes but, at other times, she put quite a lot of feeling into another popular song of the day. It went like this:

> Let him go, let him tarry, let him sink or let him swim.
> He doesn't care for me and I don't care for him.
> He can go back to his mother, for I'm sure he will enjoy,
> For I'm going to marry A FAR NICER BOY!

As teenagers, our cafe was 'The Rendez-vous' on the corner of Young Street just over the Suspension Bridge (as it was then) or 'The Ness Café' just a little bit along the street. Everyone called that side of the river, 'Over the water'. 'Down the Merkinch' was the area over the Waterloo Bridge (also called the Black Bridge) and 'Up the Hill' was the district now called the Crown district in official records. I think that the Rendezvous and the Ness Cafe were owned by the same Italian family called Gabrielli. They served us with the most delicious coffee and, when we asked for it, the assistant took a handful of coffee beans, ground them and half the enjoyment was the delicious aroma. We met friends there and our parents always knew where we were. It was there I first tasted one of my favourite biscuits – a Jacob's Club dark chocolate biscuit. I remember music used to be one of our favourite topics and one of the boys was so keen on Chopin's waltzes that I just had to listen to his raving on about them. Eventually, I came to be as enthusiastic as he was, but not as competent a player. Sometimes, if we went up town on a Saturday afternoon, we might meet one of the brothers who felt obliged to bring us into a cafe but their favourite cafe was 'The Locarno' which used to be situated opposite the bank, now in Academy Street and also had an entrance in the market. The Locarno's coffee wasn't as good as the Rendezvous, we thought, so we opted for a glass of dandelion wine which was my brother Ian's favourite cafe drink. He also used to make what we called 'Beastie Beer' which was a very tasty fizzy drink made from yeast, I think. At odd times at home we would hear popping noises coming from the larder or the cupboard in the kitchen and we knew it was Ian's Beastie Beer popping. The yeast just looked like beasties as it kept multiplying.

CHAPTER 6

'Oh, Music, come and fill my Heart's Dark Places...'

('To Music' – Schubert)

THERE is a Gaelic saying which goes something like this: "'There's plenty of food and music here", said the fox when he tried to eat the bagpipes', as the bag is usually pigskin or goatskin. There was certainly enough music and food and to spare in our house. As well as the pipes and the piano, there was a violin, a dulcimer, a mandolin, a guitar and of course the usual schoolboy's favourites – the Jew's harp and the mouth organ and the kazoo – and we often supplemented our 'orchestra' with greaseproof paper wrapped around a comb. Most of us could play a tune on those instruments.

We were all very fond of singing and had regular sing-songs round the piano. My father had a wealth of music hall songs and his *forté* was, 'The man who broke the Bank at Monte Carlo', which he sang with great gusto, twirling his military-style moustache in time to the tune. When in the Army in his younger days his pipe band used to be asked to support various artistes at concerts in many parts of the country, as this likely helped Army recruiting. He told us that he had played at Buffalo Bill's Circus and acted as a bodyguard for Queen Victoria when she visited the circus as the Camerons were considered to be HER Regiment, being 'The Queen's Own Cameron Highlanders'. I heard from other people that Buffalo Bill also visited the north of Scotland during his tour of Britain and the people who attended were thrilled to see Chief Sitting Bull and real Red Indians. I think this was all before I was born, but I have always felt it must have been a comedown from being a great Indian Chief to being a circus act. I've always likened the treatment of the Indians by the American government to that which befell the Scottish Highlanders during the time of the notorious evictions and emigrations known as the 'Clearances'. No doubt it's only now that Indians are able to read their own history through the writings of Indians in such books as *Bury My Heart at Wounded Knee.*

It was through music that my parents met. My father was a piper in the Camerons, stationed at Edinburgh Castle and he was often called upon to play piping selections at functions. My mother worked for a doctor called Keith Norman MacDonald, who had been an Army surgeon in India and was a son of Charles MacDonald of Ord, Sleat, Isle of Skye and a grandson, on the maternal side, of Captain Neil MacLeod of Gesto in Skye, who was a great authority on the bagpipes. Captain MacLeod had published a small book containing the origins and history of twenty 'pibrochs' in 1828 to illustrate the MacCrimmon system of pipe music known as '*Canntaireachd*' (Oral teaching). In his turn, Gesto's grandson, Dr MacDonald published *The Gesto Collection of Highland Music* which is considered the best of its kind ever published. My father came into contact with Mr MacDonald through the interest in piping and, as my parents both came from the same little village on the Isle of Lewis, it isn't surprising that they eventually met. My mother told me that Scott Skinner, the great fiddler, was a great friend of her employer and one of Skinner's tunes is dedicated to Dr MacDonald and is called 'Scott Skinner's compliments to Dr MacDonald'. When Skinner discovered that my mother was a Gael and came from the Hebrides, he used to ask her to sit on a chair and sing a Gaelic air … and I sometimes wonder if he incorporated some of what she sang in one of his slow airs.

Gaelic was the native tongue of my parents. However they didn't attempt to teach it to us but instead used it as a sort of secret language in the home. They did encourage us to join the Inverness Gaelic Choir though and two of my brothers took Gaelic as a subject in the Academy and, what with our summer holidays at Granny's for seven weeks or so, we soon picked up a working knowledge of Gaelic as it was then a living language in Granny's village.

We had a wonderful conductor/tutor in our choir, called Mrs Gall. Her husband was Mr John Hinton Gaul, an architect. Mrs Gall was from Argyllshire and had pure Gaelic, according to my Dad who didn't think much of the purity of the island Gaelic. The first memory of being in the choir was when I was about ten and my sister told me that there weren't enough Gaelic 'speakers' in the choir to allow them to compete at the national Mod (the annual Gaelic musical festival, similar to the Welsh Eisteddfod). Mrs Gall asked Marion and her friend, whose parents were also Gaels to bring their wee sisters (myself and Rhoda) to make up the choir numbers. We attended the practice before we left Inverness but were told not to make a sound when the choir was singing but to watch Mrs Gall's mouth and copy her, just as if we were singing. When the time came to sing at the Mod, we weren't allowed on stage until we went to a table where a man sat with a book like a chequebook and asked us in Gaelic, "What is your name?" to which I replied *"Caristiona Siosalach"* (Christina Chisholm). Then he said in Gaelic, "Where are you from?" to which I answered, *"Inbhirnis"* (Inverness). Of course we were well primed beforehand as the questions were always the same for Gaelic 'speakers'. The other members of the choir were called 'learners' and didn't have to pass a test. We were given a slip which qualified as a Gaelic 'speaker' and we had to produce this slip when we went on the stage. We didn't mind the ordeal as we had great fun during the Mod. I think the first one I attended was in Perth or Fort William around 1929 when I was ten. We stayed in a hotel and enjoyed listening to the other choirs and chuckling over their 'funny' (to us) pronunciation. No doubt the members of those choirs thought our pronunciation was just as strange However we won a lot of prizes as a choir and as individual singers in the various competitions. My brother Callum got first prize for reciting the 23rd Psalm in Gaelic and the judge, in his summing up, said that Callum was so good that, "the Gaelic was flashing out of his eyes". This made us laugh as he had learnt it in parrot fashion and didn't really understand some of the words. Mrs Gall used to translate all the songs we learned from her and it made all the difference to the expression in our singing.

Bringing a choir to a Mod in another town was quite an expensive business but Mrs Gall was an enterprising woman and would take over the Empire Theatre for a concert to raise funds. Usually, it was the normal type of concert held with some soloists, instrumentalists, dancers (The Chisholms) and the choir; I do remember she once staged a Cantata and the theatre was packed out. We were often asked to perform at concerts but what I used to enjoy were the free seats in the cinema so that we could sing during silent films with Highland connections such as 'The Lady of the Lake' or 'Rob Roy'. For the first we sang *'Fir a' Bhata'* (The Boatman) and, for the second, we sang Dorothy Wordsworth's words about Rob Roy in English to the tune of 'My Love she's but a Lassie yet'. If I remember correctly, the words went something like this:

A famous man was Robin Hood, the English ballad-singer's joy:
but Scotland has a thief as good – she has, she has the bold Rob Roy …

and it ended with the words:

… The eagle he is lord above but bold Rob Roy is lord below.

I remember that, when we were singing the one about Rob Roy, the tears came rolling down my cheeks as the film depicted Rob Roy's house being burnt down by the Redcoats.

The Gael was always in the habit of having music or song around when at work, and sometimes, when we were giving a display of Highland dancing, we would have the choir singing a *'Puirt-à-beul'* (mouth music) instead of a piper and it is difficult to keep one's feet still when listening to those tunes, most of them derived from strathspeys and reel pipe and fiddle tunes. The legend is that, when the music and dress of the Highlanders (the bagpipes, the tartan and their instruments) were proscribed after the Battle of Culloden in 1746, the only way those traditional tunes could be handed down was orally and that's how they have survived today. If you ever attend a Highland Games or an exhibition of Highland dancing and the *'Seann Triubhais'*

(Old Trousers) is included, watch it carefully. This dance is supposed to represent how much more graceful and free the kilt is as opposed to the hated 'trews' which the Highlanders were forced to wear. By the time the Proscription Act was repealed, I think the Highlanders lost heart or interest in their former mode of dress, as one rarely sees the kilt as everyday dress in the Highlands. Indeed, I remember once being laughed at in school for appearing in a tartan pinafore dress and my brothers, who regularly wore the kilt, were jeered and shouted at with, "Kiltie Danny, Kiltie Danny up the leg o' my drawers!" Later in life, I met those same people, now clad in ostentatious full Highland dress 'regalia'. There was one part of my Highland dress which I hated and that was my Inverness cape which I wore over my kilt and sometimes had to wear it on Sundays. It was a peasemeal colour and had huge batwing sleeves which I thought made me look conspicuous, whereas I wanted to melt into the background.

Once I grew up I didn't take an active interest in Highland dancing, although my sisters did and taught it in their spare time. I don't think I'd have had the patience and the only time I attended their classes was when there was no piper available and I had to play the piano and made plenty of mistakes. I was very keen on ballroom and tap dancing, which the sisters also taught and I couldn't keep still when I heard that music. We were taught a certain amount of ballroom and country dancing at school when we reached third year, probably so that we could disport ourselves properly at the school dance. I remember going home, repeating over and over again, "Step, chassis, chassis; step, chassis, chassis," after one such lesson and nearly knocking someone off the pavement in my effort to reverse the process. In my day, the boys of fifteen and under didn't wear long trousers and they all looked comical to me the evening of the school dance, all bunched around the fire in the hall, clad in black dinner suits with bow ties and patent leather shoes! They had to be prompted by the teachers to ask the girls to dance but, once started, off we went. As the evening wore on and the pace quickened, it wasn't unusual for one of the boys to swing his partner off the ground in an Eightsome Reel or the Dashing White Sergeant.

I wasn't allowed to go to other dances until I left school at nearly eighteen, except for private ones by invitation and tennis club dances in the summer. There was a young couple near us who regularly attended the annual Masonic Ball and I was invited to go with them. I don't think I danced all that much but I did enjoy the spectacle of the Grand March and all the 'Square Dancing', as we youngsters thought those were old-fashioned. I particularly liked The Lancers with its different setts and which ended up with all the ladies (me included) being whirled up high in a circle of gentlemen, with our long evening gowns swirling round. We always wore full evening dress (maxi length) when we went to a dance except in the summer to a 'Flannel Dance' where the dress would be summer dresses for the girls and Oxford bags for the boys. (No denim jeans then – those were called 'dungarees', worn only by navvies and workmen.)

When we were very young, most of the street games were singing games and we sang when we skipped or went on a swing. Dad put up a swing for us in the back green and we used to chant, while being pushed by a friend:

> *Rub-a-dub dub, three men in a tub – a butcher, a baker,*
>   *a candlestick-maker.*
> *They all went into a farmer's garden and found a rusty farthing.*
> *They gave it to their mother to buy an English brother.*
> *The brother was so cross, they bought a lily-white horse.*
> *The horse was so dandy, they gave it a glass of brandy ...*
> *And sent it off to France!*

Then we would jump off the swing. What nonsense rhymes we used to sing then. We played a game similar to the cockney 'Hokey-kokey' by joining hands in a ring and skipping round singing:

> *Hallabaloo, balay, hallabaloo, balight, hallabaloo, balay upon*
>   *a Saturday night.*
> *Put your right foot in, put your right foot out,*
> *Shake it a little a little and turn yourself about.*

Then, we all shouted 'Hooch' and continued in the same way as 'Hokey-kokey', singing to the tune of 'Lubin Loo'. When we had our sing-songs at home, the brothers used to love 'shouting songs' like 'Upidee-idee-idah', 'Bill Benbow', 'Deck the Hall' and all those songs that had to be sung with gusto; but we preferred songs like *Plaisir d'amour* (the English and French versions of which we were taught at school) and some of the Irish songs we were taught like 'My Love's an Arbutus' and we all loved Scottish songs. We had a book of 'Community Songs' containing American and other popular songs which we enjoyed singing.

One rarely sees children skipping or playing marbles out of doors. Television has taken over the role of providing outlets for children but we never seemed to be stuck for something to do. I don't hear children playing singing games nowadays but we sang as we skipped and 'cawed' (swung round the ropes) for what we called 'French Skipping'. There were so many games one could play with a short skipping rope or two longer ones, which were 'cawed' in different directions. Once a year we even took an interest in the horses running in the Derby and would crouch round the wireless to hear the commentary; and the other exciting event was surprisingly the Boat Race between Oxford and Cambridge University. I didn't know of anyone who had connections with either University but we would sit, excitedly, listening to hear whether we (the dark blues) or they (the light blues) won. There was never any money involved in our interest in those sports. The brothers initiated me into the game of cricket and we sometimes played a game we called 'French cricket', however we had no interest in cricket scores; although my teenage friend David was captain of the school cricket team and retained his interest in cricket throughout his life, whereas the brothers were 'football crazy'.

CHAPTER 7

'Schooldays, Schooldays – those were the Golden Rule days. Reading, Writing and 'ithmetic, taught by the aid of a Hickory Stick...'

(Anon)

I HAVE very fond memories of my schooldays from the time of my enrolment at Farraline Park School, through the Inverness High School and then to Inverness Royal Academy.

I don't remember my first Headmaster very well at Farraline Park (locally known as 'The Bell School' after a Dr Bell of old) but I think his name was Mr MacConnachie. I do remember his successor – Mr or Major MacKintosh, as he was sometimes called, being ex-Army. We used to chant, "The Bell School's the best school. It's made of stone and plaster. The only thing that's wrong with it is the red-headed master". Perhaps he was a disciplinarian, I don't know but he was always very pleasant when we met him in the playground and always acknowledged us in the street although I don't think he taught a class. Maybe we just sang that ditty because we had to find something to rhyme with 'Stone and plaster', and he certainly had a fine head of wavy red hair.

I liked most of my teachers. My particular favourite was Miss Wilrene MacLeod, who had such a gentle way of speaking. We used to think she was too pretty to be a teacher and unmarried! Even now, when I hear a band playing, 'Mrs MacLeod of Raasay', I'm transported back to being five years old and thrilled to be putting on my dancing pumps to dance the Reel of Tulloch because Miss MacLeod had chosen me as one of the foursome to dance at the school 'Closing', as we called the prize-giving ceremony at the end of term.

There was no such thing as PT or PE for us. It was called 'Drill' and 'Drill' it was. It was held in the playground, which was hard tarmac, on good days and in the Rose Street Drill Hall, which had an entrance off our playground, on wet days. The visiting teacher was Dan Dallas, who was a well-known athlete and weight-lifter in his day and also had a name as a singer of comic songs, some of them parodies of popular songs of that day. He made some gramophone records (where are they today, I wonder?) and our favourites were his one mimicking the Gaelic psalm singing (of which my parents did not approve) and his parody on 'Huntingtower' which went something like this:

> When ye gang awa' Jeemie, far across the sea, Laddie,
> When ye gang tae the Black isle,
> What will ye bring tae me, Laddie?

We roared at the bit when he sang … 'And when the boat begins to rock, I'll howld my bowler for ye, Jeannie'.

I don't remember much about our Drill sessions except for the memory of a squat little man with a long, red nose, dressed in yellow-brown plus-fours and brown lacing boots, skipping round the room with his hands on his hips and ourselves following likewise. Maybe he had some modern ideas as he taught us girls to play football, which we thought '*infra dig*' and we would never attend a football match but we learnt the rules of the game.

Although at the time I saw nothing special about Mr Owen, our visiting Music teacher, I now realise that I owe him a lot as he taught me in primary and then, later in secondary school. We were a musical family but our music was mostly confined to Scottish music, Gilbert and Sullivan and modern music; but Mr Owen opened up a new field to us. As well as teaching us his native Welsh songs, he taught us Irish, English and the English translations of some of the loveliest Gaelic songs, including the famous 'MacCrimmon's Lament' and 'The Mist-covered Mountains of Home'. Later on, in secondary school, we learnt from him and Miss MacKenzie (whom we called 'Singing Jess') French and German songs as well as songs from the Commonwealth – 'Maple Leaf', 'Alluetta', 'Waltzing Matilda', 'Afrikaan Trekking Song' and songs from the American Civil War. We had books of songs of Schubert, Grieg, Elgar and Handel (we were even taught words to sing to Handel's 'Largo') and we had books with a miscellany of songs. The boys in class used to deface their song-books by writing the capital letters of the word 'Preface' thus:

> *Peter Robert Eating Fish, Alec Catching Eels,*
> *Eels Catching Alec's Feet, Eating Raw Peels*

Later we were taught some arias from the operas, in an attempt to make us more appreciative of real music. One of my favourite music lessons was when Mr Owen turned the piano round and asked us to write down the solfa notes for the melody as he played. I got much practice in this and now have a habit of instinctively turning music into solfa.

One of my childhood ambitions was to become a concert pianist and, although I soon learnt that I could never come anywhere near that, I realised that Mr Owen laid the foundation for my taste in music.

The other teacher whom I remember from Farraline Park was not one who taught me in class but who introduced me to one of the loves of my life – the hockey field. Miss Robina Fraser, known affectionately as 'Robina', was a wee, dark, plump vivacious woman. Before allowing us out on the hockey field, she gave us lessons on the blackboard on the rules of the game and we were not allowed out to play on the field until we mastered those rules. I was a fanatic as far as hockey was concerned and used to enjoy the away games at Nairn, Dingwall, Tain, Elgin or Fortrose. I remember the pitch at Dingwall always seemed to be water-logged. I think they have now built the new Dingwall Academy on this site.

The teachers who stood out most from my secondary schooldays were the two who taught me Commercial Subjects – Miss Fraser in the High School and Miss MacLean in the Inverness Royal Academy. They were great friends who were always seen in town together, where Miss MacLean's family owned The Balmoral Restaurant opposite the Post Office in Queensgate.

I don't remember anyone using a nickname for Miss Fraser but we thought her beautiful as she had dark brown eyes and lovely wavy black hair and we decided that her fiancé must have been killed in the First World War, as she hadn't married. Miss MacLean's first name was Amelia and we called her that, in private of course. They both tried so hard to persuade me to go to University and take my Bachelor of Commerce Degree after I had passed my Highers but, in those days, there was nothing but teaching open for women graduates and I preferred to try to pursue one of my other ambitions – to train as a secretary and then eventually become Private Secretary to a Member of Parliament. Shortly after VE Day (8th May, 1945), I had a letter from an Inverness solicitor who said that my old boss (Mr Cameron, the Town Clerk) had recommended me for the job of local Secretary to our local MP, Sir Murdoch MacDonald as, now that the war was over, I would probably be interested in leaving London and taking a job in Inverness. I turned down the offer as I was awaiting demobilisation from the ATS and I was shocked to find that, apparently, a Member of Parliament expected me to start work for him on a date prior to my release from the Army when this restriction applied to all service personnel. Anyway, I was married by that time and was anxious to set up home with my husband when he was demobbed from the RAF as I was envious of my civilian friends who had already married and started a family. Of course, by that time in 1945, I had become rather disillusioned by MPs through attending House of Commons sittings and listening to debates. I decided I wouldn't really enjoy working for a politician.

My first shorthand lesson was the beginning of a lifelong love-affair with my shorthand notebook. This association survived well beyond my official retirement as, up until my 70s, I was still being called out to act as official Court Shorthand Writer to the Sheriff Courts in the Western Isles, Skye and the mainland. At this time it was not permissible to use tape recorders to take recordings for the official record in the Scottish Courts. It was therefore necessary to employ shorthand writers to record proceedings *verbatim* and then produce a transcript of proceedings to create the official court record.

At school, we were encouraged to practise our shorthand anywhere and everywhere and I did just that. I used to take down the words of the popular songs of the day from the wireless and type them out for my friends. Our family attended the Free North Church in Inverness and our family pew was the very back pew upstairs where, because of its high back, it was quite easy for me to hold my notebook on my knees unnoticed while I took down the minister's sermons – but I never remember transcribing those notes afterwards! When I visit Inverness, I now usually sit in the same seat and remember all the goings-on there, unknown to the people around us at that time. Callum thought nothing of bringing his two pet white mice to church. He would hide them up his sleeves and then let them run behind us up and down the pew, while Ian would pass us moth-balls in the hope that we wouldn't dare be seen looking down at them and would pass them surreptitiously into our mouths, thinking they were peppermints; and sometimes they would pull off their shoes and try to put their feet beneath our noses so that we could smell their sweaty feet! All this went on with Mother and Father at the other end of the pew, quite oblivious to what was happening at our end.

My third ambition at school was to be an author. We had no school magazine in the High School in those days, although by the time I transferred to the Academy there was one. I started writing out a few pages now and then by hand which I circulated to my friends. They consisted mostly of serial stories based on the 'Bessie Bunter' and 'Schoolgirls' Own' type of tale but I soon got fed up and stopped and no-one else seemed to want to help. Somehow, my friends seemed to think I was an authority on ghosts, probably because my parents were Hebrideans and I was constantly being asked to tell a ghost story. Some I remembered having heard when on holiday at Granny's but others I just made up as I went along for the purpose of seeing their eyes widen. So much for my ambition to become an author! Through the years I have had some articles published in magazines and have had a couple of short stories broadcast and the local newspapers have asked me to write book reviews.

My best friends at school were two 'chums' whom I first met when in my pram. They were Ruth and Rene. Ruth was on my class at school but Rene was a class lower – by age not by intelligence. We three went to school together and, although I had similar interests as both of them, they didn't have the same interests as each other. When they both left school at 15 and I went on to the Academy I made some new friends, but I regarded Rene and Ruth as my best chums, as we kept up our friendship throughout our lives. Rene eventually became a working colleague before the Second World War and Ruth became a working colleague in my time at Cameron Barracks when we were both called up two days before war broke out in September, 1939.

During our schooldays, we were taught love of our country. Was this a bad thing? Looking back on my war experience, I think of the futility of war, where only politicians and armaments manufacturers gain anything, but I know that we all went into it because of the love of our native land. Almost half of the boys who were in my class at school never came home again. At our Assembly in the mornings we sang hymns and patriotic songs like, 'Land of our Birth', 'Land of Hope and Glory', 'What Service Shall we Render Thee', 'I Vow to Thee my Country' and 'Who Would True Valour See' and I go along with Sir Walter Scott when he asks, 'Breathes there a man, with soul so dead that never to himself hath said, "This is my own my native land …"' Later in life, when an officer in the Girl Guide movement, I was astonished to find that none of the children knew the national anthem, remembering how we used to have to stand to attention whenever we heard it played at public functions. We respected our teachers and rather looked up to them. Perhaps now the values of my generation are looked on as being old fashioned.

I've kept one or two souvenirs of my schooldays (I'm well-known as a hoarder) and one of those is my autograph book. Nearly every schoolboy or girl at that time had such a book but it wasn't used to harass famous people (we didn't know any famous people anyway!) for their autographs. We passed it round our friends and acquaintances, who wrote rhymes and witticisms in our book. One of my friends wrote, 'Love many, trust few, always paddle your own canoe' and another wrote, 'He who fights and runs away will live to fight another day but he who loves and does not wed will find himself in court instead'. The latter was signed by one of the boys in the street – my friend David – who put all sorts of legal qualifications after his name at the age of fourteen or so. In time David did grow up to be prominent in the legal profession. Of course the brothers had to wreak havoc with my book. Someone had written, 'Christina Chisholm is her name, single is her station, happy is the lucky man who makes the alteration'. This was too much for Callum, who once, sneaking the book away, wrote the letters 'un' before the words 'lucky' and 'happy', just to keep me in my place. At other times, the brothers would condescend to write some lines after their own names as they also had autograph books; but their taste inclined to be on the gloomy side, for instance, 'When I'm dead and in my grave and all my bones are rotten, this autograph will bear my name when I am quite forgotten'.

I left school in May 1936 and in December of that year there was a great sensation in the land. King Edward VIII, the former Prince of Wales, whom Marion said she was going to marry, was found to have feet of clay and abdicated. There was great excitement in Inverness with everyone listening to the radio bulletins and going to Inverness Railway Station for hand-out 'Stop Press' notices from the daily newspapers. I don't know where the idea came from but I was asked to copy a verse that someone had composed about the crisis and it went round all the offices in Inverness. I came across a copy in an old scrapbook and it went like this:

An Idyll of a King

There was once a little Monarch who sat upon a Throne
And as he was a bachelor he sat there all alone.
He tried to find a lady to sit along with him
So one day he doffed his cady to a girl called Mrs Sim.
Said he, "I'm very lonely upon my golden throne.
My dear, I want you only just for my very own.
I know you're over forty but I am forty-three
And though they say you're naughty,
Well – that's OK by me".

Said she, "Alas! I'm married but my husband is a clown.
How I wish I'd tarried for I'd love to wear a crown".
The little Monarch looked annoyed then said, "I know a man
Who'll make your marriage null and void" – so off to court they ran.
The Judge put on his wig and gown and said "The case is clear.
Your husband bars you from a Crown – I'll soon fix that, my dear".
He straightway granted a divorce, ne'er asking for causation
And timed it to come into force before the Coronation.
Then the lovers were elated and fixed the happy day
When they would be mated with none to say them 'Nay'.
Just then the voice of Stanley B. rang out so stern and clear,
"You may do that in the USA
... BUT YOU CAN'T DO THAT THERE 'ERE!"

We young folk felt very sorry for the royal lovers but, with hindsight, Edward appeared weaker in this and in his dealings with the Nazis during the war. The abdication was to prove a blessing in disguise and, when the real test of kingship came during the war, King George VI and Queen Elizabeth were an inspiration to us. I quite often saw them down among the ruins after a particularly heavy bombing raid on London, speaking to the bereaved and the air raid wardens and other helpers.

CHAPTER 8

'The Blue Islands are Pullin' me Away and Laughter puts the Leap upon the Lame'

(Rev Kenneth MacLeod)

C HILDREN today are so far travelled that crossing the Minch means little to them, but to us it was an exciting journey and was part of our Great Adventure – the start of the school holidays on the Island of Lewis in the Outer Hebrides or, as we used to call it, '*Tir-nan-Og*' (The Land of Eternal Youth or the Gaels' Paradise). We got up at the crack of dawn to catch the Kyle train from Inverness and watched our two cabin trunks being loaded onto the taxi. I can remember the time when it was Mr Handford, the Inverness cabbie, with his tile hat and a long whip at his side which he never seemed to use on his sleek horses. There was also a largish case with odds and ends for the journey but, in those days, one didn't have to worry about luggage once it was put in the guard's van. When we got to Kyle, we stood on the pier to ensure that our trunks were loaded on board the steamer in the string-bag net, which must have been very strong, as it even lifted the cars on deck. There was no such thing as roll-on/roll-off ferries then!

Once aboard the train we recited the stations we had to pass and knew them all off by heart, although the names the porters shouted on the platforms as we passed through seemed to bear no resemblance to the spelling on the notice boards. The carriages were clean and comfortable and there was always a dining-car on with an attendant coming along and opening each compartment door and shouting, "First call for Lunch" (sometimes there were second and even third calls for lunch) but we made do with tea and sandwiches. I loved to sit by a window and watch the changing scene but my brothers would walk along the corridor, sometimes leaning on a window, whistling or singing Gaelic airs or bagpipe tunes, their fingers moving in time on the window-bars as if they were pipe chanters. Anyone who looked suspicious we thought was bound to be a German spy or a Stuart activist coming to see if the Highlands would respond to a call for another Jacobite rising. There were few cars on the road and we couldn't play car numbers but we played 'First Good Luck a White Horse', which had to be shouted whenever a white horse came in view. We then had to run and touch wood while we shouted but, as I was always slow in coming alert to the fact and that someone had already shouted, 'First Good Luck a White Horse', the brothers usually scored first, second and third and, as there was no fourth 'Good Luck', I was called a dreamer.

I was told that I first crossed the Minch as a baby on the *Sheila* but my memories are of the *Loch Ness*, the *Loch Seaforth* and the *Suilven* which ran from Kyle. We were all good sailors and loved the seven hour journey over the Minch and the variety of sea-birds we saw on the crossing. For a while, there was always a dolphin accompanying us as far as the Sound of Raasay but I heard it was killed by a boat propeller. Particularly exciting was watching for the little rowing boat which came out from Applecross on the west coast of Ross-shire to ferry passengers to our steamer, as that was the only means of communication between the Applecross peninsula and the mainland in those days, although there is a winding road to get there now. We watched with bated breath the way those passengers, sometimes holding a baby, stepped gingerly from the rowing boat into the hold of the steamer where all the cattle were and we wished we could have had such an exciting adventure. Incidentally one of my Gravir Chisholm cousins (Ian Chisholm) settled in Applecross after the war and used to be the oarsman on the Applecross rowing boat.

My father wouldn't trust any porter to carry the rectangular wooden box containing his beloved bagpipes and carried it himself. Once somebody guessed the contents of the box, he would be persuaded to play and, before long, the deck would be crowded with young men and girls dancing an Eightsome Reel. I think, at that time, there were lots of young folk returning from fishing ports and jobs on the mainland to help to cut the peats, etc. for their parents; and many of those girls would outshine today's glamour queens. The dancing would go on until we reached the Shiant Isles where the legendary 'Blue Men of the Minch' rocked the boat furiously and grounded most of the passengers, some of whom rushed to the rails to be sick. We thought all this was hilarious as we had earlier seen some of them sitting in the steerage with whole cooked chickens and ducks on their knees, sharing them with their friends. Even that didn't dampen spirits as there was always someone ready to sing a Gaelic song and the boat would resound with the chorus. I remember hearing some of the Gaelic songs which are still sung today being sung on the steamer when we were crossing the Minch.

When the boat arrived in Stornoway, the quay would be jam-packed with people, as in those days it was the only means of transport to and from the mainland. Certainly the plane and the ferry boats nowadays are more convenient and comfortable with the shorter journey.

By the time we squeezed past the throng on the pier and reached the bus it would be after 10 pm. The Connemara bus hadn't a look in on our bus and sometimes it would be so full that it would be choc-a-bloc in the aisles with someone perhaps holding a garden rake and someone else with a circle of wire strung around a dozen herrings or haddocks.

There was no breathalyser in those days but the drivers were very sensible on the whole and didn't take chances on such single-track roads. However, there was always the maverick driver who would have a friend standing beside him with a half bottle of whisky in his hand, helping him to 'swig' from the bottle at regular intervals until it was empty. There were no cattle grids and each village was surrounded by a drystone dyke with gates at the extrance and exit. Usually one of the passengers got out to open and close the gates to save the driver trouble but I know of one driver who thought nothing of charging through the wooden gates if he couldn't be bothered getting out. I heard that, one night when his headlamps failed, this particular driver made two youths sit on the bonnet with torches to light the way home. The bus stops were many and varied as passengers disembarked and locals came to collect their 'messages', have a chat with the driver and a look into the bus to see who was there. I remember one 'message' was a copy of the *Stornoway Gazette* wrapped round a bottle but it fell with a crash into fragments on the ground, with the golden liquid spilling out. As the accident happened when it was changing hands, there was a great hullabaloo between the driver and the local as to who should pay for the smashed bottle. This went on with each protagonist getting more red in the face and their voices raised higher until the driver reached behind his seat and withdrew another half bottle and handed it over with a laugh. He had filled the first bottle with cold tea, just for the fun of seeing the effect on his customer for the loss of the weekly dram. No-one worried about the clock in the Islands then and nobody seemed to object to the hold-ups on the way. Once darkness fell there was nothing to be seen but the twinkling lights of the houses dotted here and there, but when the sweet aroma of peat filtered through the bus, it gave us a bout of the '*ciannalas*' (nostalgia or homesickness) and we longed for Granny's peat fire flame.

It was midnight before we arrived at Granny's and climbed up the hill to her house. Inside would be lit with an 'Aladdin' tilly-lamp and a blazing peat fire. Sitting on what she called the 'chaise' (a long, wooden bench) would be our next-door cousins waiting to welcome us and probably waiting for the presents Mum had brought. When I first went to Granny's at Gravir my older cousins had to interpret as we had no Gaelic and the younger cousins had no English. Once they went to school they spoke perfect English and we had learnt some Gaelic.

The journey homeward to Inverness was never as eventful as the outward one, as the steamer left Stornoway at midnight and, apart from going up on deck to bid farewell to our Loch Odhairn, shimmering in the moonlight as we passed Kebbock Head, we slept until we came to Kyle and then slept on the train to Inverness.

However, there is one homeward journey that I shall never forget. That was at the end of August, 1939, a couple of days before the outbreak of World War Two. The steamer was bursting at the seams with uniformed men, mostly Royal Naval Reservists and the whole population of Lewis seemed to be standing on the quay at Stornoway. Just as the boat was slipping her moorings, someone on shore gave out the first line of a Gaelic psalm and soon there was an enormous crescendo of voices from the shore and those lining the deck, rather reminding me of stories I'd heard about the sinking of the *Lusitania* and the *Titanic*. It was even more poignant as we passed the Beasts of Holm near the entrance to Stornoway harbour where over two hundred Lewis servicemen were drowned, when they were returning from war service in the early hours of New Year's morning 1919.

I heard some years later that that night in August 1939 happened to be the time of the Communions when Stornoway was crowded with churchgoers from all over the island. Apparently the singing was heard that night all down the coast to the Eye Peninsula. Tragically, many of those who accompanied us on that night, including some of our teenage friends, never again made their homeward journey to Lewis but joined the ranks of that 'lost generation', who gave their 'today' for our 'tomorrow'.

We enjoyed every minute of our holidays in Lewis and the days were too short for us. However, we gained an extra hour-and-a-half in the evening by putting Granny's Westminster chimes clock half-an-hour slow and, as she refused to conform to British Summer Time, her clock was always an hour slower than Greenwich. I don't know if she guessed but she didn't seem to mind us coming in at about two o'clock in the morning, knowing that we had probably been at a *ceilidh* somewhere in the village.

Even the everyday work on the croft was a source of fascination for us and we all wanted to help in our small way. I liked to tease the wool on the carders while my granny sat at her spinning wheel. I also liked to hammer the plunger up and down in the butter churn and make butter pats for the table. Blanket washing was done by going to a loch where a big three-legged iron pot was heated on top of a brushwood or heather fire. We then trampled the blankets with our bare feet in big wooden tubs and then helped to spread them out on the hillside to bleach for a week or so. Bringing home the peats was another source of entertainment for us and sometimes we would stop to watch a weaver at work in his home or be lured towards a house by the sound of women's voices raised in a '*Puirt-à-beul*' while waulking (shrinking) the Harris Tweed they had woven.

There were plenty of places to spend our Saturday pennies – four shops – but our favourite shop was 'Donald Moyle's' shop where we were presented with a choice of jars of sweets of all colours. I was intrigued with the articles hanging from the open hatch of the loft – pairs of wellingtons, ropes, women's overalls and brown corduroy knickerbockers (worn by most of the local boys with navy-blue Guernseys). I would have loved to explore what was in that loft and, according to Donald Moyle's' son, who became my husband, there was everything in that loft from the proverbial needle to an anchor.

My older cousin Nina could make any excuse for a picnic on the moor beside one of the numerous lochs in our area, which was called South Lochs or Pairc. She used the most beautiful china cups for our picnics and would have looked askance at our present-day coffee mugs. I remember saying to her once that we wouldn't go for a picnic that day because the wee man in Granny's weather house was out and that meant rain. Nina just said, "Well, we'll just have to push him in again …" She did just that and we went on the picnic, believing the rain would stop because the man was pushed back into his 'Doo-cot'.

Sometimes we would go beachcombing, mostly for wee crabs to keep as pets in a basin or to put in our brothers' beds. We were forbidden to swim in the sea, but who needed a swimming-pool when the hulk of the old *Delight* lay full of water at the head of the quay just below Granny's house in Gravir Bay. We could dive right into the hold from the gunwales.

As teenagers we were bitten by the fishing bug and Loch Odhairn would be full of young people hunting the fish – and what a variety there was. I have a photo of myself, aged eighteen holding up my catch of a huge halibut. In spite of almost daily fishing during my early retirement in Gravir, I have never again caught a halibut and everyone says that's because the trawlers come into the loch and net all the fish.

We used to bring a portable gramophone on our fishing trips and records of the great Gaelic singers of those days and sometimes we would anchor at a bay near the head of the loch and climb the hill, where we would light a heather fire and have a picnic.

In the evenings, we would go to bring the cows in and then wait for the rallying call of the melodeon at the '*Aridhmhor*' and join the throng for '*Danns a Rathaid*' (The Dance on the Road). Not that there was much dancing done there, it was more in the nature of a rendezvous for young folks. We used to go around in fours, usually the crew of our rowing boats, being two girls and two boys and we would then adjourn to a house where we would have an impromptu *ceilidh* and listen to spine-chilling ghost stories and hilarious tales of local characters. One of the locals was referred to as 'J.R.' as those were his initials but the locals pronounced them as 'Chy R.' He wasn't in the least like the famous villain 'J.R.' of the television series 'Dallas', although he could spin a yarn. We believed his tall tale about having been present at what he called 'The Battle of Culloden Muir' – but that was all in fun, as we later realised.

Sundays weren't as boring as people were led to believe. If it were a good day after dinner at mid-day, we would go up the hill above Granny's house and lie in the sun; if it rained we collected our next-door cousins and all gathered round cousin Nina who taught us to sing the rousing Moody/Sankey hymns and Salvation Army choruses. We went to church twice a day on Sundays and didn't seem to mind that all the services were in Gaelic, as we met our friends afterwards and, in the evenings, all the young folk met at the cross-roads for a chat.

I think we learnt quite a lot about life from being present at a *ceilidh*, a Gaelic word for a foregathering of friends; my Granny's house was often the venue for such. In fact that Gaelic word *ceilidh* has now become absorbed into the English language to mean 'a visit', and people often say, "I'm going to ceilidh on Mrs ..." In the evenings in Lewis most houses would have a quota of visiting friends and neighbours and that would constitute a *ceilidh*. All we had to do was walk through the ever-open door, squeeze ourselves into the chaise below the window and sit there, all agog, listening and absorbing everything we heard. There would usually be a flow of conversation interspersed with laughter and gentle teasing and sometimes, but not always, a song, perhaps a humorous one composed by the singer about some contemporary event or about one of the local characters. I don't recall seeing strong drink being passed around during those *ceilidhs*, the refreshments on offer were often milk, whey and strong tea – 'The cup that cheers but does not inebriate'.

The *ceilidh* topics ranged from local incidents and traditions to politics and tales of foreign parts. It was hard to believe that the *'Fear an Taighe'* (Man of the House who usually acted as master of ceremonies), puffing contentedly at his pipe of black twist, had sailed round the world; or that his 'cailleach' ('old woman' but often used instead of 'wife') had worked in marble halls in big cities or the Americas. She might be sitting serenely knitting or spinning, just as if she had never left home. The atmosphere was more like a family gathering because all ages were represented and there was no feeling of the generation gap.

We young folk didn't take much part in the conversation but, for me, it was a sort of school of life, as we learnt a lot from our elders. All the talk was in Gaelic, which for me, made it more exciting, as the Gaelic words seemed more expressive than the English.

One of the most frightening stories I heard discussed at a *ceilidh* house away back in those days was when one of the *'bodachs'* ('old men' but also 'husband') declared that, if there was another war with the Germans, we would all be wiped out as the Germans had developed a 'death ray' which would shine and melt everything and everybody on impact. This must have lodged itself in my subconscious mind because, a few nights afterwards, I had a terrible nightmare about a war and that someone was shining the death ray on my face.

When I woke up, terrified, I discovered it was only my brother Callum shining his torch through the window on his way home from a late-night fishing trip. Surely, that story of a death ray between the two World Wars must have been a prediction of the laser beam? A lot of the stories told round the peat fire at the *ceilidhs* were about ghosts and the 'Second Sight'. There was one experience I remember which might have qualified for a ghost and that was when I was coming back to Gravir with a friend after having visited relatives in a village a few miles away. Just before we descended the hill leading into Gravir village, we sat for a few minutes to rest on a little hillock near the roadside, by a little loch where we could see for miles around. After a few minutes I became conscious of hearing voices but my friend said she could hear nothing and, anyway, there was no sign of anyone. I then heard a regular sort of metallic clang, but again my friend heard nothing. I turned my ear in the direction of the sound and I saw a man, clad in blue dungarees, jacket and trousers and wearing a cap and he seemed to be digging intently at a place about ten yards from me with a pickaxe. I couldn't see his face but I saw the pickaxe he was using. I was so surprised that I shouted, "Hello," but he disappeared ... and still my friend saw nothing! I felt slightly foolish about this and told nobody until I got back to Inverness and told my mum. Mum asked me where exactly I had seen this 'ghost' and, when I described the place, she said, "People have been seeing things there for years". When I asked her to elaborate on the things she said she didn't really know except that there was talk of people seeing ghosts there. The thing was that what I had seen was not in the dark of night but on a clear afternoon about five o'clock. I wasn't frightened as I immediately thought it was a 'photograph' of something that had happened at that spot at some time or other – or else I was seeing a man who was actually digging over the Minch at Lochinver and, by some unexplained means, his actions were being reflected on our side of the Minch. This idea was reinforced about forty years later when my husband's brother told me that he had been going fishing and had to walk past the same place with his fishing rod to get to a trout loch, when he had seen a woman in a long white gown coming towards him over the heather. He wondered where she had come from and where she was going to in, what he thought was her nightgown, when she suddenly vanished into thin air. He told me he got such a fright that he immediately turned round and went home. This sighting was also in the afternoon. Only then did I mention my experience and to me it seemed as if people were seeing different visions at this spot. All this was before the advent of television but I wonder if that particular spot contained a sort of natural aerial, which could pick up pictures and transmit them? Perhaps a ghosthunter would say that the man who was digging killed the woman in the long gown and then buried her at that spot.

My sister Marion had an even more strange experience during a holiday in Gravir during the 1930s but she was always very reticent about mentioning it for fear of being ridiculed. One evening while out with a cousin for the cows, they took shelter from the rain near a loch when, 'Lo and Behold', a shower of fish fell from the sky. The fish were alive when they fell and were about three inches in length and they were all herring. Some fell on hard ground and were killed but others fell on soft ground and survived. The fish didn't fall helter-skelter everywhere or here and there. They fell in a straight line, not more than a foot apart. At first Marion didn't want to tell Granny in case she was accused of telling fibs but, when she did mention it, she was amazed when Gran just shrugged her shoulders and said, "Och, that was just 'Sgadan Atha'r'" (Air Herring) but we had never heard of this. We had heard of 'Sgadan Ur' (Fresh Herring), which the fish sellers shouted in the streets of Inverness but we had never heard of 'Sgadan Atha'r' – so Dad was consulted when we got home. Dad didn't bat an eyelid and said that, although it wasn't all that common, there had been reports of people seeing things other than rain coming down from the sky and asked us hadn't we heard of it raining cats and dogs? He went on to say he had never really heard of cats and dogs coming down, although he had heard of it raining frogs. We thought he was just in fun but, years later, I read about frogs and fish being reported coming down from the sky in different parts of the world. Dad told us that, the next time we brought our sledges up to the golf course and passed through Fluke Street and the Fluke Inn there at Culcabock to look at the sign on the street and above the door of the Inn and we would see an entirely different name than 'The Fluke' as that was only a nickname given by the Invernessians after a shower of fluke (flounders) had come down from the sky there many long years before. I think the correct name of the Inn was 'The Culcabock Inn', but I recently saw a new sign over it, re-named 'The Fluke'.

I read in a book that even as far back as Pliny, there are reports of frogs and fish descending from the sky and a probable explanation was given that they were swept up from their natural habitat by a whirlwind and then deposited somewhere else; but some people disputed this, maintaining that the fish they saw fell from a clear sky.

As we grew older, others in the family began to go elsewhere on holiday but, except for short trips to Aberdeen and the south, I always spent my annual holidays in the Hebrides and retained my love of island life, eventually settling there.

CHAPTER 9

Career Girls and the Mystery of the Disappearing Coronation Chocolate

B Y THE TIME we were fifteen, Ruth and I decided that we were going to be career girls and wouldn't get married until we were at least thirty!

I had worked sometimes during the school holidays at the telephone switchboard at a local hospital and in the office of a seedsman but I set my sights on working in a 'proper office'. As soon as I sat my Highers in the required subjects – English, Literature, History, Maths, French and Commerce, which included book-keeping, accounts, business training, commercial arithmetic, stocks and shares, typewriting and shorthand – I decided I was going to look for a job; but my parents weren't keen on my leaving school until I had actually passed my Highers. My mother said that if I failed, I would have to go back to school to try again and she said I had plenty of time anyway as I was only in fifth year. In those days there was no such thing as exams at 'O' Level. We sat what were called 'prelims' which, if you passed, made you eligible to sit for Highers. You couldn't get your Higher Leaving Certificate if you didn't pass in Higher English, no matter how good you might be in other subjects and if you failed any of the subjects you sat, you had to resit the whole lot again. One of my teachers told me that I was lucky, as, although I had passed all the other subjects with good marks, I had just scraped through my Higher French. It wasn't surprising that, when I went to France, no-one seemed to understand what I was trying to say.

Some people seem to have a natural flair for languages but I don't have that gift and even today, after a lifetime of speaking and studying the Gaelic language, I make some awful mistakes and my pronunciation is often a source of amusement.

I was determined to get a job if I could, as my parents were not well off, there were no such things as grants and I felt I wanted to become a little more independent. So I watched the newspapers and when I saw a job advertised for a Junior Shorthand Typist in the Town Clerk's Office, I applied. I had almost forgotten about my application when I got a letter stating that there was to be an examination paper set for twenty-four applicants in the High School, Inverness. One of the Baillies in the Town Council was the ex-Headmaster of the High School and he had arranged this and was the invigilator during the examination. He had probably also set the questions. The only question I remember from that paper was the last question, which is still being asked today, 'What do you think of the Palestinian Question?' What indeed! I knew nothing about this and so filled in my answer by detailing all I knew about the Arabs and then what I knew about the Jews and then ended by stating, 'As Sir Roger de Coverley would say, "Much can be said on both sides"'. After an interview with the Town Clerk, Mr James Cameron, I was engaged to start work and that was the beginning of my working life. It was months afterwards before we got the results of the Highers and, fortunately, I had passed. Even if I hadn't passed, I don't think anyone would have forced me to go back to school as I was enjoying so much being one of the world's workers.

When I started work, I must admit that I thought I knew EVERYTHING about business life but, after the first day in the office, I realised that, apart from some theory, I really knew NOTHING about the practical side of business. My first surprise was being ticked off for sticking a stamp upside-down on a letter and I was told that this wasn't a polite thing to do! I then got instructions about how to address letters to the 'County' folk and the titled folk who were being invited to a civic reception. I didn't feel outraged by this but looked on it as part of my training. However when it came to addressing the Chief of the Clan MacKintosh as 'The' in front of his name I refused to do so, as my father had told me that the only Clan Chief entitled to put 'The' in front of his name was our own Clan Chief, The Chisholm of Chisholm, in terms of the old Gaelic proverb that, 'There are only three "The's" in the world – The King, The Pope and The Chisholm'… so I addressed MacKintosh as 'MacKintosh of MacKintosh' without the 'The'.

Everyone in the office, from the boss downwards was very kind to me and my immediate colleagues – Miss Margaret MacRae, Miss May Fraser (who, in later years became Town Clerk Depute) and Miss Ismay Gordon – treated me like a younger sister and I gladly lapped up all the instructions and advice they gave me. Although those three ladies all did shorthand, my boss often asked me into his office to take dictation and Mr MacKenzie-Reid, the then Town Clerk Depute, sometimes gave me legal documents to type. It was the best way to learn as I had all sorts of jobs to do – the mail, reception and any odd errands round the other council offices or solicitors' offices in the town, together with the tea-making. The ribbons in our typewriters were of indelible ink because, although we always took carbon copies, by law, we had to have exact copies and this was done on a thick tome called the 'Letter Book'. The pages were of flimsy paper and I had to soak two fabric cloths in a rectangular bath and then place them, one on each side of the letter and close the book. The book was then put in a letter-press which had a screw for pressing it down. Every letter had to be treated in this way and I had to write up and index the letter book so that it was up-to-date and ready for inspection at any time. This is a long way from the computers and filing of today but we had undisputable proof of all our correspondence via the letter-book.

When I saw the huge new office of the Highland Tourist Board being built in Inverness, I had to chuckle to myself as I remember that it was my job to send out guide books of the Highlands to all those who wrote in for information regarding holidays. In those days it was more the huntin', fishin', shootin' type of visitor we had, rather than tourists of today. Those guide books were as thick as a paperback and had lots of information about our area and the north and west, as well as articles about the Highlands written by such well-known writers as Seton Gordon. Later on, when the tourist mail got very heavy a Tourist

Officer was appointed but, as we had no room for him in the office, he sat on a chair with a table full of brochures and leaflets in a small space between the outside front door and the inner glass door of the Town Hall. From such humble beginnings great industries grow! I played my own small part in its early days.

Mr Cameron was known as the best boss on the council and, although I was slightly afraid of him (I was rather a shy person and he had a high standard of expectation), he was always kind and considerate to us. Sometimes, during municipal and general elections, he would let me off for the day to act as an Enumerator or a Clerk or Presiding Officer to make extra money and, even after I had left business to bring up my children, I would be sent an offer of an appointment during the elections which was a great boon to me. In later life, when I lived in the Islands, my past experience helped me to get similar jobs at elections.

We were told that, when a member of the Town Council came to the office and wanted to chat, we were to stop what we were doing and attend to them. I think it is my memory of those councillors that influenced me against party politics in local government and also against the payment of local councillors, except for travelling expenses and loss of earnings. The Inverness town councillors of those days were all men who had made a success of their own lives, or were public-spirited enough to care about the common good of their town.

Around the time leading up to the Coronation of King Edward VIII, the Inverness Town Council decided that they would have to give a presentation to school children in the Inverness area to commemorate this grand occasion. We in the Town Hall took delivery of a load of boxes, each containing a large number of smaller tin boxes, adorned with a picture of Edward VIII, the length of a pencil case and containing several squares of 'Coronation Chocolate'. These were safely stored in the strongroom of the Town Clerk's office. After all the schools in the local area had been given their allocation, there was still quite a number of tins left over in the strongroom. On 6 December 1936 a constitutional crisis arose and Edward VIII announced to the nation that he was to abdicate, declaring his love for Wallace Simpson, an American divorcée whom he wished to marry. As a result

Callum, Chris and Alex (*l–r*), Farraline Park School, 1927

Alex (*l*), Chris and Marie (*seated*), and Jack,
Farraline Park School, 1930

Chris (*back*) and sister Marie,
Innes Street, Inverness, 1926

Pipe Major Malcolm Chisholm
with son Kenny and daughter
Marion, Gordon Castle,
Fochabers, summer 1926

Chisholm children waiting for the Stornoway bus
in Gravir, 1934 (*l–r*) Callum, Chris, Alex, Jack, Marie and Paddy

Chris in school blazer,
Innes Street, Inverness, 1932

Chris in back garden,
45 Innes Street

Inverness High School Hockey Team
(*Chris far left back row, friend Ruth holding cup on left*)

Chris's Auntie Lena, cousin
Nina and Granny Macphail,
19 Gravir, Isle of Lewis

Malcolm and Johan Chisholm,
Chris's parents, Innes Street

Chris's maternal granny's home, Croft 19 Gravir, Isle of Lewis

Postcard of Gravir, with Chris's granny's home, Croft 19 (*upper left*)

Chisholm family and friends, Innes Street (*back left*) father Malcolm,
Marie, Vi Macdonald, Callum, mother Johan, Ian, Chris, Cecil
Maclennan, (*front l–r*) Alex, Paddy

Chris in ATS uniform,
Loch Ness, 1938

Chris and Don catching halibut,
Loch Odhairn, Gravir, 1938

ATS 'Terriers', Cameron Barracks, Inverness before outbreak of war,
June 1939 (*back l–r*) M Mitchell, friend Agnes Watson (later Love),
M Fraser, (*seated*) Chris, F MacGregor and C Duncan

No. ...of B690 35. Army Form E. 511H.

AUXILIARY TERRITORIAL SERVICE
NOTICE TO JOIN

Surname _CHISHOLM_

Christian names _CHRISTINA, JESSIE_

Address _45, INNES STREET,_

INVERNESS.

In accordance with the conditions of your enrolment you are
hereby required to present yourself at the Headquarters of your

Company _40ᵗʰ Inverness Coy. A.T.S_

You should therefore report at _Depot A. O. Cameron Hgʳˢ_

on _Sept. 1ˢᵗ_ not later than _8 a.m._ o'clock
bringing this notice with you.

If your Health Insurance Contribution Card and/or Unemployment Book are in the possession of your employer or of the Employment Exchange, you should obtain them, if possible, and bring them
with you. But IF YOU ARE UNABLE TO GET THEM YOU
MUST NOT DELAY JOINING ON THIS ACCOUNT. If you have
to apply to the Employment Exchange for your Unemployment
Book, you should take with you the Receipt Card (U.I.40) and this
notice.

If your Unemployment Book is with the Exchange and you
cannot get it, you should bring the Receipt Card with you instead
and hand it in on joining.

You will receive travelling expenses from your residence.

Pay at the rates in force for the A.T.S. will, if retained for full-
time service, be issued.

M. C. Fraser Signature.

Date _31/8/39_ _____ Rank.

Place_____ _____ Appointment.

Chris's Calling Up Papers to report to Cameron Barracks,
Inverness, 1 September 1939

Chris 'under escort' while
training, Cameron Barracks, 1939

Chris, Innes Street, 1939

Ruth and Chris, childhood friends
and ATS girls, 1939

Barracks' concert party The ITCATS (Infantry Training Centre and ATS),
1940 (*l–r*) Chris and dancers Gray, Forbes, Duncan, Graham and Mackenzie

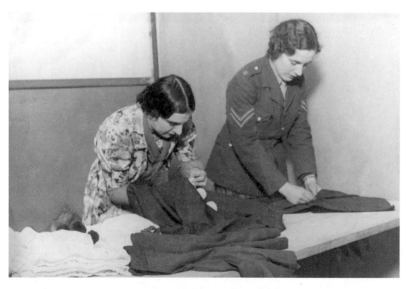

Mrs Pope the bandmaster's wife and Chris preparing costumes for
ITCATS concert party, 1940

Sgt Chris Chisholm, Yard 10
Ardross Terrace, Highland
District HQ

Ruth Sharp, childhood friend,
joining ATS, 1939

ATS friends Joan, Ruth and Molly, picnic near Inverness, 1941

Chris, sister Marie and friend
Rene on a trip to Aberdeen, 1939

Chris with brother Ian

Chris, Ruth and CRE Highland District HQ pet,
Craig Dunain, Inverness, 1941

Sister Marion marries Bill Mackenzie with Chris as bridesmaid,
30 September 1937, Strathness Hotel, Inverness

Engagement of Corporal C J Chisholm ATS to Leading Aircraftman
Donald Morrison RAF, 1939, Inverness

Sisters Marie and Chris Chisholm, 1942

Chris with friend and ATS colleague Margaret Fraser, February 1943

Picnic in Hyde Park, London. Chris (*left*) and War Office colleagues
Joan Horner and Shirley Hay, 1943

Chris and Donald's wedding, Inverness, 15th October 1943

Bride Chris in her ice-blue 'going away' outfit, 1943

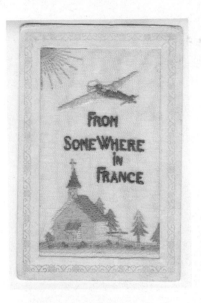

Embroidered card sent to Chris by husband Don serving in France

LAC Donald Morrison RAF, Chris's husband

Career girls Joyce MacDonald and Chris, Inverness, 1938

Chris's friend and ATS colleague, Joan Davy, marries Captain
Charles (Chuck) T Horner Jr, US Army (later Major General Horner)
at Colchester, Essex on 14 May 1945

Already serving with Territorial Army, Chris and brother called up to
Cameron Barracks two days before war broke out, September 1939
(l–r) Alex, Jack, Chris and Ian

PART I

INSTRUCTIONS TO RELEASED PERSON

MEDICAL TREATMENT AFTER LEAVING MILITARY DISPERSAL UNIT

You are now entitled to medical benefit under the National Health Insurance Acts, and a medical card telling you how to get treatment will be sent to you as soon as possible.

Medical benefit includes free treatment from an insurance doctor at his surgery (or if your condition requires it, at your home), and free medicine.

If you go back to live in your old district and had an insurance doctor before you joined up you will be restored to his list if he is still in practice himself or by deputy.

If you fall ill before the medical card comes, fill in the application below and hand this book to your previous insurance doctor (or, if absent, his deputy). If you did not have an insurance doctor before you joined up or if you go to live in another part of the country, apply to any insurance doctor. You can see a list of insurance doctors at the local Post Office.

Do not detach the form from the book. The doctor will do this.

PART II—To be completed in Unit

Form Med. 50A

Military Dispersal Unit Stamp

Rank ....Pte/W.O.II........ Number ....W/13890...............

Initials ....C.J......... Surname (Block Letters) ....MORRISON.........

Date of Birth ..20 . 2 . 1919.. Sex ..FEMALE.. (If a married woman, state maiden name) ....CHISHOLM......

[stamp:] MILITARY DISPERSAL UNIT No. 1 ★ 19 JUN 1945 ★ EDINBURGH

The above-named individual left this Military Dispersal Unit on the date shown in the stamp opposite.

PART III

Available for three months from date of leaving Military Dispersal Unit.

To be completed by released person ONLY if needing medical treatment before a medical card is received.

I have NOT received a medical card since leaving the Military Dispersal Unit and I hereby apply for a medical card to be issued to me.

Delete as may be necessary { I was on the list of Dr...immediately before I was mobilised or called up for service.

I was not on the list of a doctor in the district where I am now, and I desire to be placed on the list of.............................

My present address is .... (Insert name of doctor or approved institution.)

Do you intend to leave this district within three months from the date hereof ? If so when ?...........................

Name of Approved Society* (if any)...........................
(If a deposit contributor write " D.C.")
Name of Branch (if any) of Society ....

Membership number........................... (Signature of released individual.)

Date...........................

* If you were a member of an Approved Society before you were mobilised or called up for service, or if you joined an Approved Society during service, your membership is still effective. (See also overleaf.)

Military Dispersal Form, June 1945

of the abdication, there was no coronation for Edward VIII and it was George V who was crowned. In the meantime all the remaining chocolate tins remained at the Town Hall and could not be distributed, as they depicted the uncrowned Edward VIII. One day Ismay, the senior shorthand typist, said to me, "There's still that Coronation Chocolate in the strongroom, what's going to be done with all these chocolate boxes? What do you say …?" (I'm putting the blame on her, but I should say it was a joint endeavour). After some discussion, we decided that we would remove one tin, so we took one tin and divided it between us and put the empty tin back in the strongroom. Oh, how delicious was that chocolate, I can taste it now! This pattern of consumption went on for a few months. Eventually of course I was posted to London to work at Whitehall and so left Inverness. However on my return home on leave on one occasion I asked Ismay, "What's happened to the Coronation Chocolate, is it still there? Have you eaten any more of it?" Ismay said "Oh yes!" and every time I would go to visit her after that, she would bring out some more of the Coronation Chocolate and we'd have a feed of it. Between the two of us we finished the lot! The Town Clerk must have thrown out all the tins once he discovered they were empty. No-one else ever knew the mystery of the disappearing Coronation Chocolate!

My own favourite Councillor was Baillie Joseph MacLeod, the father of my favourite teacher, Miss Wilrene MacLeod. I think he was actually the Liberal agent for the north of Scotland and he was a great supporter of the 'Crofters' Rising' which had culminated in the passing of the Crofters' Act of 1886. Baillie Joseph, as he was familiarly called, had written some pamphlets on the crofter question, but he never let his Liberal politics interfere in regards to the good of the people of the town of Inverness and he was typical of the other members of the Town Council, some of whom were 'characters' in their own right. I can't remember if it was 'Sesha' or 'Scourguie' but one of those farmer councillors always insisted in bringing his collie dog into the council chamber when he attended meetings. The Invernessians are almost as prone to bestowing nicknames as the Hebrideans and it is the nicknames which I tend to remember.

Baillie Joseph liked to try out his native Sutherland Gaelic on me but sometimes his Gaelic stumped me. He once asked me, when I returned from Lewis, "Did you find a Gaelic sweetheart when you were on holiday?" At the time, I had met my future husband, Don, and I told Baillie MacLeod that I had indeed met a Gaelic sweetheart. He said, "That is good. Gaelic is the language of love. You have only to remember all the words in Gaelic for 'love' and the different terms of endearment. You are very fortunate!" Indeed, thinking about it, he was correct and, if the Greeks have a 'word for it', I think the Gaels have two! Baillie Joseph was a kenspeckle figure in the streets of Inverness and dressed very elegantly – he wore a grey homburg, a grey three-quarter length topcoat, with white gloves and white spats. He always carried his walking stick and he had a silver grey beard to match his clothes.

When I had been very happily settled in my job for about eighteen months, Miss MacRae took me aside one day and said to me she would like to have a heart-to-heart chat. 'What's this?' I wondered. She said she noticed that I was very ambitious as I had gained RSA certificates at school as well as Highers and had gone to night school to get my HND in Commercial Subjects. (What she didn't know was that I was taking a correspondence course from a secretarial college). Miss MacRae said that she thought I would gain nothing career-wise by staying on in the office, as she and the other two girls would block my promotion and, although I would get annual increments, I would still be regarded as the junior. She was around forty at this time and said she had no intention of marrying and she didn't think it fair to keep me unaware that there wasn't much prospect for promotion as she thought May and Ismay probably wouldn't marry either. However, she was only bringing the subject up as she had been seconded to attend the council chamber to take notes of meetings in connection with a new government office that was to be set up in Inverness – the office of the Northern Regional Council for Physical Training and Recreation (or commonly called then, the National Fitness Council), set up under the Physical Training and Recreation Act of 1936. Miss MacRae had discovered that they would want a competent shorthand typist, she thought the job would suit me and that, being Civil Service, it might lead to greater things. Would I apply?

I felt sorry at the thought of leaving my friends in the Town Clerk's office, but I went to my boss to see what he thought and although he said he would be sorry to lose me, he quite understood the position. I applied for the job, was appointed and was ever grateful to Miss MacRae for her advice. Nevertheless, I never lost touch with my colleagues and my boss in the Town Clerk's Office and I always made a point of visiting them for a chat during the war when on furlough and when domestic circumstances permitted, Mr Cameron always managed to recommend me for any part-time position that suited my circumstances ... so it was a very amicable break. I was asked what I wanted for my farewell present and I chose a camera and Miss MacRae presented it to me, with the infamous 'Jess Going-To' poem.

I didn't really need to get caught up in the 'Keep Fit' fever that was sweeping the country then, as I was always an outdoor girl and, when we couldn't go for a hike or a cycle run, we would always find time to play tennis, hockey, badminton or dancing to keep us fit.

The Northern Regional Committee of the National Fitness Council consisted of a dedicated body of people. They were all very keen on the idea of the 'Keep Fit Movement'. Our Chairman was Colonel Harry Houldsworth of Dallas, Forres and there was Lady Hermoine Cameron of Lochiel (the mother of the Chief of the Clan Cameron), Mrs Gooch, Banavie (well-known for her good works), Kurt Hahn (the founder of Gordonstoun School) and his assistant Dr Zimmerman, together with others who had some authority in the area.

My boss was an ex-Seaforth Highlander – at that time a Major but he later became a Brigadier – James E. McConnel, known to his friends as 'Johnnie' but we called him 'The Jem' because of his initials and because we always found him a perfect gentleman. There was a clerical staff and a few organisers who travelled the country areas in the Highlands in an effort to interest everyone in 'Keep Fit' with a particular emphasis on building village or community halls, for which purpose we arranged grants available through the Council of Social Service, etc. Coming from an Army family I know there is a great feeling of camaraderie among ex-Servicemen and I wondered if there was a sort of 'Old-boy' network in the Army similar to the 'Jobs for the Boys' for ex-Public schoolboys. This was because most of the male staff and some of the Regional Committee were ex-Army, mostly from the Seaforth Highlanders, which wasn't our County Regiment, although the Cameron and Seaforth and Gordon Highlanders have now been amalgamated, much to the regret of those who have connections with all three regiments. One of the exceptions to the ex-Army personnel was a family friend who was a Bailie in the Town Council – Mr J.D. MacDonald, a connection of Marion's husband, Bill 'J.D.', as he was familiarly known, had retired from business in Inverness but was quite influential in the sphere of the council. 'J.D.' was one of our organisers and he and I used to have a laugh at the peculiar-sounding (to us) names in the west and in the Hebrides. I had had experience of Skye and Lewis names but I was quite amused to hear of such places as Bualnaluib and Claddach Kirkibost, where we had appointed voluntary representatives to further the aims of the Movement. Someone on the staff said he thought some of the Gaelic names, like Achiltibuie, sounded like swear words and, as none of us used swear words, we sometimes substituted 'Achiltibuie' for one when we were annoyed.

At the time it was decided by the powers-that-be that I should have an assistant, Rene was looking for a job; so I made the 'Bell School' network operate and recommended her for the vacancy. This was the beginning of a wonderful working partnership which lasted until I went to the Forces in 1939. Rene did Pitman's Shorthand, whereas I did Gregg's and throughout my working life I have never worked with anyone who wrote Gregg Shorthand – it was always the Pitman system they used. My teacher, Miss MacLean could teach both systems but she recommended learning the Gregg system. She told us that at one time, the government would employ only Pitman writers because it was a British system and Gregg was supposedly American and also because, if a Senior Shorthand Writer had to leave some transcription to attend to more immediate matters, a subordinate could take over to read her shorthand. I find this hard to believe as, over the years, one devises certain outlines and brief forms of one's own and I don't think anyone would ever be able to transcribe my scrawls. Miss Maclean also maintained that it was wrong to say Gregg was American. He was British (I think Scottish) and had gone to America to patent his system because Pitman's had the monopoly in this country. By the time I started work, the Civil Service didn't seem to care what system was used as long as it could be transcribed properly.

The 'Keep Fit' Office was at 33 Academy Street on the top flat above the Rodmure School of Dressmaking and Fornari's Hairdressing Salon. We didn't calorie count in those days and the fact that we were situated right opposite Burnett's Bakery and Tea Room did nothing to help our figures! We had a weakness for cream and marzipan cakes – even on our way home we would buy a cake to guzzle when walking up Strother's Lane. Our Chief Clerk, 'Paddy' Heffernan, also an ex-Seaforth was a good sort and very helpful, with a great sense of humour and most of the others were of the same sort but we had difficulty sometimes in extracting the one shilling a week 'tea money' from some of the male staff.

The pay was almost double what I'd been earning before and, as we got paid weekly instead of monthly as in the council offices, the money seemed to go further. The work was very interesting but in a different way. I had to attend the board room meetings, taking minutes and writing to our members, keeping them up to date with what was going on. At our inaugural meeting in the Empire Theatre, Inverness, everyone in Inverness seemed to be present to hear the speakers, one of whom was Miss Prunella Stack, whose mother had founded the League of Health and Beauty. I have a memory of my first glimpse of Prunella as the very epitome of a lovely British girl, exuding an aura of good health. There were several groups of the League in the Highlands and it was more popular than the straight 'Keep Fit Exercise' type of thing, as the League concentrated more on music and movement, with more of an aesthetic effect. We envied Prunella her good looks and coveted the sort of fez hat she wore at that first meeting.

I'm not sure whose idea it was; I'm inclined to think it was a brainchild of Kurt Hahn, but plans were made to set up a 'Summer School for the Training of Youth Leaders' in June, 1938. Advertisements were placed in all the papers asking for applicants for places and we sent out forms to all the youth and voluntary organisations in the area. Arrangements were then made for speakers and instructors and it was decided the school would run for a month, with courses of fourteen days, so that as many people as possible could attend. Lady Aberdeen kindly gave permission for us to use Guisachan House, Glen Affric in Chisholm Clan country which is one of the most beautiful glens in the Highlands, situated off the Inverness/Beauly Road. Lord David Douglas Hamilton, one of the sons of the then Duke of Hamilton, was appointed Warden in charge of the course and he later married Miss Prunella Stack, who was also on the staff. I don't remember all who staffed or lectured at Guisachan but I do remember that most of them were well known in the 'Keep Fit' world. Lord David's brothers attended but I can't remember whether they came as guests to observe and take part in the course or whether they spoke to the trainees. The Duke of Hamilton of that time was well known for his interest in the 'Keep Fit Movement' and his eldest son, the then Marquis of Douglas and Clydesdale, had made a name for himself by flying over Everest. Later, during the second World War, when the Marquis had succeeded to the Dukedom, he was astounded to find Rudolph Hess, Hitler's Deputy, stepping out of a plane on the Hamilton Estate and demanding to speak to him. Another name I remember was that of Jock Hunter, who later ran Glenmore Lodge (perhaps a product of 'Guisachan') and 'Freddie' Spencer Chapman, the famous mountaineer and explorer who, I think, was teaching at Gordonstoun or at Robert Gordon's College at the time. We had also been in touch with Sir John Boyd Orr of the Rowatt Research Institute, Aberdeen, who later became Lord Brechin and was the foremost nutrition expert appointed to the United Nations – so, even in those far-off days, our Committee had made the vital link between being fit and healthy eating.

I was not involved with the running of the school except for the initial paperwork but I sometimes went up with 'The Jem' to type a few letters for Lord David. Sometimes we had to visit Kurt Hahn at Gordonstoun and Mr Hahn once asked me if I would like to see round the school. Even in those days the school had a distinguished reputation and I was astonished to see the spartan conditions in the boys' dormitories, as there were no shades on the light bulbs and just bare boards on the floors. I remember once witnessing a hockey match with the then Prince Philip of Greece, now Duke of Edinburgh, in the team and he cut a fine figure with his quick movements and his fair hair.

I was told that Kurt Hahn was a German who had fled to Britain when Hitler came to power, as he had become *persona non grata*. He set up Gordonstoun School on the same lines as he had done at Salem in Germany. Hahn believed in the challenge of the outdoor life and competence, compassion and high endeavour. When he founded the Outward Bound Movement in 1941 he is supposed to have said, "I prefer the lawless to the listless", meaning, I suppose, that he preferred people to meet life's challenges. Away back before 1941 he had started the nucleus of the Outward Bound Movement in the area around Gordonstoun with various schemes for young folk to help the community at large. Indeed I often thought, when confronting problem children while acting on the Children's Hearing Panel, that I'd like to send them off on one of Kurt Hahn's courses, to work off their aggression. Perhaps in material terms life is easier for young folk today but perhaps they drift into trouble because they haven't faced and overcome a challenge. Our challenge was probably the war of 1939-45. Kurt Hahn's assistant, Dr Zimmerman, had come over from Germany with him. He was some kind of financial expert and he worked out most of the financial arrangements for the school.

Although it had first been thought that Guisachan places would be reserved for those in the Highland area, it was decided to give places to some people in the Lowlands, with the result that there was a good cross-section. One of the girls from the Perth area composed a song during the last ceilidh held at Guisachan and it was sung to the tune of 'Horo, my Nut-brown Maiden' and the chorus went like this: 'For love, for life, for laughter, it's Guisachan for me'. We arranged to have a picture of Guisachan mounted on a card with the Guisachan song on the reverse as a souvenir of the first summer school. Guisachan was probably the forerunner of today's adventure schools as Glenmore

Lodge was set up after the war by the Council for Physical Recreation. Of course we had no glossy brochures. Everything had to be typed out and run off on the Gestetner duplicator. Glen Affric was an ideal location for outdoor adventure and pursuits and, in the evenings the impromptu ceilidhs were considered great fun, with Lord David playing his bagpipes, his brother Lord Malcolm playing the accordion and everyone joining in the fun and sing-songs.

We hear that young people now complain about having nothing to do; I wonder why? They have TV, and often youth clubs and sports halls, etc. I would think there were more opportunities to kill time than we had – and yet the day never seemed to be long enough for us. We spent the summer months out of doors and, in winter, we played badminton, went to the cinema or the theatre or visited each other's houses. Rene lived a few doors up Innes Street from me and Ruth lived in Victoria Square, now the multi-storey car park off Rose Street. Girls then used to prepare what we called our 'bottom drawer'. This was supposed to be in preparation for marriage and usually consisted of embroidered linen – tablecloths, traycloths, tea cosies, etc. In spite of our being keen on being career girls, we too were able to have a bottom drawer when we married; and we did quite a lot of knitting and sewing during the winter evenings. Rene's parents were Plymouth Brethren and didn't believe in going to the 'pictures', nor did they believe in uniformed organisations; but Ruth and I, once we were earning a wage, went once a week to the pictures. We liked Ginger Rogers and Fred Astaire films but our favourites were murder mysteries and horror films. I wasn't keen on Dracula films as I have a phobia about birds and bats. I love birds and feed them daily and, while I don't mind them walking close to me, I am terrified of them when they fly and flutter near me and I can't bear the feel of their feathers. When in London during the War, I used to keep a wide berth between me and the pigeons when going from my office in Whitehall to Leicester Square to my favourite vegetarian restaurant there. This phobia even covers the eating of chicken and game as it gives me a shiver. I don't know the cause of this as my mum said she had never been chased by a bird! Frankenstein films were favourites too but, when time to go home arrived, I would be so scared that I would ask Ruth to come down Innes Street with me; and then she would be so scared that I would have to go up Innes Street with her and then wait until one of the brothers came along and saw that we both got home safely. Of course we liked the romantic films as well and had a good weep over Greta Garbo in 'Our Lady of the Camelias'. (Camile.)

My introduction to the theatre was by way of attending the evenings held in the LMS Railway Scout Hall when my brothers were Scouts. The two officers there were real theatre buffs and, believe it or not, I saw 'The Ghost Train' and 'Sweeny Todd, the Demon Barber of Fleet Street' produced by them on the Scout stage. They were both in the community drama team and were good actors and, when I met one of them later on in life in Skye, many years later, he was still involved with community drama. There was a theatre on the riverside in Bank Street in Inverness when I was quite small and I believe they had had visits from good professional touring companies. I remember my brother telling me about seeing 'Phantom of the Opera' there but, by the time I had started theatre going, it had been burnt down. This caused quite a stir in Inverness at the time as people thought it was because of a prediction by the Brahan Seer who had said that, "When a theatre in Inverness was built between two churches, it would be burnt down by fire ...". The theatre was situated on the riverside between the Free North Church and the St Columba Church.

After the Inverness Theatre was burnt down, the venue was the Empire Theatre in Academy Street but we weren't so keen on the variety shows that were mostly performed there and, when a local Repertory Theatre was set up, we went once a week. They called themselves 'The Little Theatre' and performances were held in the old Raining School at the top of the Raining Stairs off Castle Street although when Farraline Park was closed down as a school, 'The Little Theatre' moved there. The repertory company consisted of a band of dedicated actors (with one or two locals in the cast) led by one Ronald MacDonald Douglas, who at that time owned the Bogroy Inn on the Beauly Road. I remember going to see, 'All Quiet on the Western Front' and 'Journey's End' there shortly before the war broke out in 1939. Ronald MacDonald Douglas was supposed to be an ardent Scottish Nationalist and the programmes were headed 'The Little Theatre' in Gaelic. Once war broke out, the company dispersed and, as far as I know the Inverness Repertory Theatre was never resuscitated. The annual drama festivals continued over the years, as they do today. The most famous local team, 'The Florians', are also still flourishing. The only teacher in Bell's School who gave me 'the strap' was at that time one of the leading lights in drama and was a superb actress – but she could fairly whack with the strap!

Everything seemed to be going smoothly in 1939 and, although Guisachan wasn't available for our summer school, because I think the roof had been removed due to an issue about rates, we were offered Gordon Castle, Fochabers, which was larger and more adaptable. Most of the same staff, speakers and instructors were engaged and everything proved so successful that plans were being made for a repeat the following year when, to put it bluntly, Hitler stepped into Poland and knocked all our plans off course! Not only were our plans upset but our whole world changed and life after 1945, when the war ended, took on a whole new dimension for the people of the Highlands and the world.

A few days before war broke out on 3rd September, 1939, the boss and most of the staff, including myself, were called up to the Forces. By that time I was in the part-time Territorial Army called the 'Women's Auxiliary Territorial Army' (The word 'Women's' was dropped and the initials ATS were used). I was on the Reserve List and was called up to Cameron Barracks on 1st September, 1939. We had previously heard from central government to pack up all our 'Keep Fit' papers and prepare for a takeover by the National Food Office (Ministry of Food) with jobs for all. As it happened, Rene was the only member of the clerical staff left to take over from me and she stayed for the duration of the war under a new boss – a retired manager from the Ministry of Labour. Mr Urquhart was a competent and popular boss and, in fact, came to my rescue when I first reported to Cameron Barracks and was given an ancient Oliver typewriter which looked like a Heath Robinson contraption, with keys coming out of each side, almost at eye level. I begged the use of one of the Imperial typewriters and

Mr Urquhart kindly lent it to me until the Army eventually indented for a modern machine.

Thus ended the halcyon days of youth for me and my generation and we had to concentrate on playing our part to win the war against evil and aggression.

PART II

GOING TO WAR

CHAPTER 10

'This is the Army, Mr Jones – no Private Rooms or Telephones...'

(wartime song)

B Y THE TIME I turned twenty-one in 1940, none of my brothers were able to attend my birthday party, as they were all away from home, serving in the Forces or in reserved occupations. I myself was serving in the Women's Auxiliary Territorial Service.

After the meeting between Hitler and Chamberlain in 1938 at Munich, it was decided to form a corps of women reservists rather like the WRAC in the First World War and so the ATS came into being. The Northern Area was commanded by three 'County' ladies; Lady Maud Bailie of Dochfour (mother of Lord Burton), Mrs Fraser-Tytler of Aldourie Castle, Dores and Mrs Charity Fraser of Reelig, Kirkhill.

I didn't know Mrs Fraser-Tytler before my ATS days but I knew Colonel Neil Fraser-Tytler her husband slightly as he was on the county council and sometimes he used to fall asleep during council meetings, because he had caught sleeping-sickness whilst serving in Africa. I used to know many of the 'County' ladies through my job, particularly around the times of civic receptions for VIP visits, such as The Prince of Wales (Edward VIII) when everyone would call at the Town Clerk's office to see if there was an invitation to the VIP receptions. However during that period, the 'County' ladies of that era were very public-spirited and I remember Lady Hermione Cameron of Lochiel; Mrs Cameron Head of Inverailort; Mrs Gooch, Torecastle, Banavie; Mrs Smyth, Ness Castle; and Laura, Lady Lovat were all on various committees devoted to the Common Good.

They had no premises but central government advised our office in Inverness (the Northern Regional Council for Physical Training and Recreation or National Fitness Council) to make a room available for those ladies for their meetings and for their files. We had a suite of rooms but the only room we could find suitable was the board room. The ATS stored their files in the board room and my boss, Major McConnel said that, if I wished, I could help them with typing, which I did.

One day Major McConnel had said to me, "Miss Chisholm, you are getting nothing for all this extra work you are doing for the ATS and, although you already get three weeks' annual holiday from the government as a civil servant, if you joined the ATS yourself, you would get another fourteen days to go to camp with them in the summer". I discussed this with my parents, who didn't mind either way. I then talked it over with my friend and colleague Rene who wasn't interested in joining but my friend Ruth was very interested. Ruth and I joined early in 1939 as we thought it was a great idea to get an extra fortnight's paid holiday … so it was self-interest rather than patriotism that made me join in the first place. However I am certain that I would have volunteered anyway, once I saw the list of missing friends from the ranks of the 51st Highland Division in June 1940.

At that time Inverness was a garrison town for the county regiment, The Queen's Own Cameron Highlanders (the 79th). Fort George housed The Seaforth Highlanders (the 78th – the "Ross-shire Buffs", the Ross-shire County Regiment). These regiments have now amalgamated with others to become the Royal Regiment of Scotland. We saw soldiers in the streets of Inverness but we never seemed to come in contact with them in ordinary life, except for some of the pipers who had Lewis connections or those who came to my dad for piping lessons. Like the folk in Kipling's 'Tommy', people tended to look down on soldiers and we wondered how we were going to get on with 'Tommy Atkins' when we were told to report to Cameron Barracks instead of going away to camp. We were told that some army reservists were being called up and that we would be allocated jobs which would be our duties if and when a real war broke out. Ruth was sent to the Quartermaster's stores to give out uniforms and I was sent to the Orderly Room to search out the paybooks of former regular soldiers who had served their time but were still on the reserve list.

It was an eye-opener to us to find out that soldiers were no different from other boys and were a cross-section of the population in 'Civvy Street'. We soon made friends and my colleague in the orderly room happened to be a piper who had known my eldest brother Angus in India. He sometimes played for my sisters' dancing classes – he himself eventually became a Pipe Major – so we had many a laugh together over the attitudes of some of the reservists – some genuinely patriotic and some (like Ruth and myself) in it for the money and a holiday!

By this time we had a khaki uniform and were measured for beautiful worsted tartan skirts in Ancient Cameron tartan, which was much more colourful than the Cameron of Erracht tartan worn by the Cameron men. Mrs Fraser had supplied us with special Cameron brass buttons for our uniforms but shortly after war broke out we had to remove those on the instructions of the War Office and replace them with ordinary GS (General Service) buttons, much to our annoyance.

After our fortnight at the barracks we continued to report there every week to do regular 'square bashing' under the watchful eye of Colour Sergeant Adams, who sometimes shouted at me, "Chisholm, keep your head up and your shoulders back. I've already lifted up all the threepenny bits from the square!"

All the same, Ruth and I didn't pay much attention to politics in general and continued blissfully unaware of the implications of our enrolment in the ATS. That all changed when, returning from a holiday in Lewis with my fiancé Don at the end of August, 1939, I found my sister Marie at the barrier beyond the Kyle train, with my calling-up papers asking me to report at Cameron Barracks on 1st September, 1939, which turned out to be two days before war broke out. Being a civil servant, I expect I might have been able to wriggle out of military service due of the takeover of my office by the Ministry of Food where

I had been offered a senior position but I never thought of such a thing. I'm very glad I did not, as I would have missed out on the whole experience of being in the wartime ATS.

I don't think that at the time we realised how critical the war position was but I do remember being very moved when I witnessed the departure of the 4th/5th Cameron Highlanders (Territorials) from Inverness. The words Ewart Alan MacKintosh wrote about the departure of the 4th/5th Camerons from Inverness at the time of the Great War sometimes haunt me when I remember that time in 1939. MacKintosh was from Tain, Ross-shire and was killed at the Battle of Cambrai in 1917. His words were as follows:

> *The pipes in the streets were playing bravely,*
> *The marching lads went by,*
> *With merry hearts and voices singing,*
> *My friends marched out to die;*
> *But I was hearing a lonely pibroch*
> *Out of an older, older war,*
> *'Farewell, farewell, farewell MacCrimmon,*
> *MacCrimmon comes no more'.*
>
> *And every lad in his heart was dreaming*
> *Of honour and wealth to come*
> *And honour and noble pride were calling*
> *To the tune of the pipes and drum;*
> *But I was hearing a woman singing*
> *By dark Dunvegan shore,*
> *'Farewell, farewell, farewell MacCrimmon,*
> *MacCrimmon comes no more'.*
>
> *And there in front of the men were marching,*
> *With feet that made no mark,*
> *The grey old ghosts of the ancient fighters*
> *Come back again from the dark;*
> *And in front of them all MacCrimmon piping*
> *A weary tune and sore,*

'On the gathering day, forever and ever,
MacCrimmon comes no more'.

Three of my brothers, Alex, Jack and Ian were playing in the pipe band on that fateful day, which for most of us proved to be the end of the days of carefree youth, although none of us realised it at the time.

At first, at the Cameron barracks, everything was a 'hoot' and we didn't have Army ranks. I had been given two stripes (the same as an Army Corporal) but was called a 'Sub-Leader' (formerly my rank was 'Volunteer').

It wasn't surprising that we soon used Army ranks. We were a novelty as far as the men were concerned and they treated us with amusement, but with respect. Although there were some civilians employed at the barracks, we were the first women to serve there and sometimes we felt as if our contribution to the war effort was considered one great joke. There was however a great demand for shorthand-typists, no doubt to save some of the less diligent officers from having to write everything in longhand. I felt vindicated when I organised a combined team of First Aid Nursing Yeomanry, who wore similar khaki uniform but were employed as drivers, and ATS. My good friend Agnes Watson (later Agnes Love) played alongside me on that day. We gave a good beating at a hockey match against a combined team of Camerons and RAF servicemen stationed in the town.

CHAPTER 11

Keeping Fit

ALTHOUGH I was keen on playing sports I wasn't keen on gymnastics. I was therefore not very pleased when Mrs Fraser approached me and said that, as there were as yet no PT instructors in the ATS she thought that I should spend one afternoon a week instructing PT since I had been connected with the 'Keep Fit' Council in my former job. I told her I had no qualifications or experience for this work and had just worked on the administrative side. Nonetheless she furnished me with a booklet with 'matchstick men' illustrations of PT exercises and, with a memory of school gym, I somehow managed to give an hour of PT. Some weeks later, I managed to solve the problem by suggesting that we should have PT from Sergeant Blake, the Camerons' PT instructor, and he acted until one of the girls was sent on a PT instructor's course.

A similar sort of thing happened when a concert party was formed, probably crediting me with more ability than I had, owing to my connection with our family dancing displays. The concert party was to be called 'The ITCATS', incorporating the initials of Infantry Training Centre and ATS. This troupe was for the purpose of entertaining the troops at the barracks and around the Highland area. The officer in charge of entertainments approached me to do the choreography for the dancing members. He probably knew my brother and my father and the fact that some of the pipers often played for our dancers who were taught tap-dancing and other novelty dancing as well as Highland and Scottish dancing. I did what I could from my memories of the old musical films but I refused to do a solo act, preferring to be a member of the chorus, which I enjoyed very much and when not on stage I helped the bandmaster's wife with the costumes. Some of the other girls did solo parts and looked very glamorous in long evening gowns under the spotlight (especially Hester with her burnished red hair), singing such popular songs of the day as, 'I'm all for you, Body and Soul' and 'My Heart Belongs to Daddy'. Pat, with her slim figure and blonde hair led the chorus and I chose as the opening number, 'I Want to be Happy', from 'No, no, Nanette'. We had great fun in the chorus, kicking up our legs and imagining we were as good as the girls in the Moulin Rouge or the Folies Bergere.

Later on, by the time the Entertainments Officer had been posted to France, 'ENSA' (the concert party formed nationally to entertain troops) provided entertainment with companies from the south and we had visits from well-known entertainers ... so that let us off the hook!

I remember Harry Lauder being billed as coming up to the barracks and, although we didn't like the way he caricatured the Scots (and particularly the Highlanders, speaking with broad Scots accents instead of a Highland lilt), we felt he was a good trouper and worth seeing. The day before he was due to come up, one of the civilian maintenance staff told me that he had known Harry Lauder very well in former days and had, in fact, written some of Lauder's songs – particularly 'Roamin' in the Gloamin''. I was sceptical but he showed me several printed postcards with his name, Neil MacFadyen, printed below the songs he had written. One was dedicated to Queen Mary during the first World War and she had written an acknowledgment on the bottom. I think Mr MacFadyen was perhaps a painter as he always wore white overalls and was too old to be in the forces. He said he would probably go back-stage to see Lauder after the concert but, when I saw him afterwards, I more-or-less understood he hadn't been given a very warm welcome by Lauder. I wasn't really surprised to hear this, as we were all rather put off Harry Lauder from that time onwards because during the concert he complained about the noise made by some of the young fellows who were sitting at the rear of the hall. He stopped in the middle of a turn, saying he refused to go on until the noise stopped. We hadn't been conscious of any noise but we knew that the occupants of the three back rows were the first batch of militiamen who were due to leave for France the next morning and they were probably a bit excited. We resented Lauder's attitude – especially when word came through later that some of those boys had been killed in action. The result of all this was that I never forgot Neil McFadyen's name because, every time I hear an announcement about a song supposedly composed by Harry Lauder, I find myself asking – "… or was it by Neil MacFadyen?'"

Ruth and I cycled home for lunch but we had a hut where we gathered for our elevenses and a chat and a sing-song round the piano, with Jenny Matheson at the keyboard. I always associate the song 'One Day When We Were Young' with this period in my life. I think it was from a film called 'The Great Waltz' based on the life of Strauss and it seemed to epitomise our idea of romance. Eilidh Bethune and Agnes Love saw to it that we were looked after in our hut and it didn't surprise me to learn that after the war Eilidh became a hospital almoner as she had such a caring nature and came from a family of chemists and doctors. Agnes married one of the Regular Camerons on the staff at the barracks but shortly after the end of the war, she was left a widow with three young children to bring up on her own. However, Agnes did an excellent job of it. One of her sons made his name in the Nature Conservancy Council with the re-introduction of the sea eagle into the island of Rum and her other two sons went into journalism.

Initially I refused to work on Sundays as it was against my principles and I suggested that some of the civilian staff might like to do Sunday work, as they would be paid overtime and may jump at the chance. My boss (an Army Major) gave me a lecture that the men at the front couldn't stop work on Sunday and the women in factories had to work Sundays and we couldn't afford to relax the war effort if we wanted to win the war. I gave in and never complained of Sunday work after that, the object being to do my bit and to get the war over as quickly as possible.

The bagpipes were heard everywhere in the barracks. Instead of the bugle, Reveille was played on the bagpipes with 'Hey Johnnie Cope, are ye Waukin yet?' For lunch the tune played was 'Loch Arkaig' (to which the troops sang, 'Come for your rhubarb and custard!'). For teatime, the tune was 'Bundle and Go' and 'Lights Out' was 'Sleep, Baby, Sleep' to which the men sang 'Johnnie, lie down on your wee pack o' straw. It's not very neat and it's not very braw'. Sometimes a most awful cacophony could be heard from the band hut on the other side of the square where Pipe Major ('Pipie') Young was instructing his young pipers – a lot of them later becoming Pipe Majors in their own right. The ones I remember mostly were Captain John (known as Ian to us when he played for our dancers) MacLellan, who later was in charge of the Army School of Piping at Edinburgh, Hugh Fraser (later of the Scots Guards), Evan MacRae, Malcolm MacPherson (son of the famous Angus of Invershin) and I think John Burgess turned up at the barracks about the time I was being posted away from there. 'Pipie' Young also taught Highland dancing and ticked me off once for jumping too high when doing the *pas-de-basque*. He told me that that was all very well for exhibition dancing but looked most unladylike in a ballroom. So, from that time on, I tried to remember there was a difference in that Highland dancing was more of a celebration of a victory over one's enemy and not suitable for a ballroom. After that on most occasions I danced a very decorous Eightsome Reel, except when the sett was composed of fellow Highlanders, when we all danced with our usual leaps and loud 'hoochs'.

CHAPTER 12

Army Training

THE TIME CAME when Headquarters for the Highland area were set up in Inverness in hotels and other requisitioned quarters and I was promoted to the rank of Sergeant and posted to work for the CRE (Commander, Royal Engineers). The staff were a mixture of uniformed and civilian personnel and I had a small typing pool of five civilians. The staff under the Surveyor of Works consisted mostly of civilian draughtsmen, clerks of works and architects and there were only a few Royal Engineer soldiers in uniform, as even the pay office was staffed by civilians, some of them women. My boss was in civilian life the head of a firm of Aberdeen architects and although I found him pleasant enough, I found the work pretty tedious at times. Most of the work was in connection with the fortifications in the north of Scotland and sometimes I had to take long lengths of shorthand dictation in the form of bills and specifications from the Surveyor of Works. Those were passed to the surveyors' clerks for 'squaring the dimensions'. I used to admire the way they managed to fill in the columns using the duodecimal system, about which I hadn't a clue! In fact many years later in Skye I came across one of our civilian surveyors' clerks of those days busily engaged in the hotel trade in Skye.

There was a good team spirit in the CRE's Department and if we were working late some of the boys in the office would arrange to come in with chips for us, with perhaps a wee bottle of 'pommie' – a fizzy drink not unlike champagne. The draughtsmen also saw to it that we got some of the blue linen paper they used for plans which we took home, boiled the starch out of it and made it into embroidered tray and supper-cloths! The Colonel's batman, Henry MacPherson, was a Cameron Highlander who for some reason hadn't been posted with his regiment to France. His folk had a farm at Stratherrick and he used to contribute eggs to our diet at home. Almost everything was rationed in the way of food and clothing and although I enjoyed the hens' eggs Henry brought us, I didn't like the goose eggs we sometimes got from him – a single one would have filled a frying pan and fed four from one egg!

The Colonel's driver was an Aberdonian who spoke with a thick Doric accent and we had difficulty in understanding him, as he used some very expressive words like "Fit's adae?" for "what's up?" The Major's driver used even more expressive words when he was in the pit trying to find out what was amiss with the car engine; but I was the only one who recognised that Tommy MacInnes had a good supply of Gaelic swear words! Tommy was a Skyeman who could sing a beautifully haunting Gaelic melody while busily working at the car and it made me nostalgic for the walks I remember under a Hebridean moon.

I think I was fortunate that in every office I worked in my colleagues were very friendly and had a good sense of humour. I found this was also true in army life and we were always playing tricks on each other. I remember one episode at CRE's office when I was sent a cheeky poem by one of the boys in the finance department. He had seen me at the railway station saying goodbye to my fiancé Don on his returning to duty with the RAF. The poem was full of cheeky references to 'The Brylcream Boys' (nickname for the RAF in those days) and praise for the boys in khaki. I couldn't very well say anything derogatory about khaki as I was also dressed in it but when the poem called my Don 'big ears', I was determined to get my own back. Army personnel were good at evading payment to the tea fund, but sometimes we would treat each other to buns as there was a bakery nearby. We girls decided to 'treat' the boys to some buns but to fill them with 'Brooklax' (laxative chocolate) in retaliation for their cheeky poem. We had a good laugh about it until another poem appeared, beginning, 'We do not think it is great fun to put some Brooklax in our bun'. I think we must have forgotten to erase the trade name on the chocolate! However, there was no bad feeling in the office and if our civilian Chief Clerk (who had a glass eye and called 'Wylie Post' by staff) knew what we'd done, he didn't show it.

One day, while chatting to our administrative subaltern, I told her I felt the work wasn't all that important and could be done by a civilian. The officer I spoke to on the subject was a local girl – Gillian Mitford from Lentran (later Lady Charles Troughton). I explained to her that I would rather do something worthwhile but that there didn't seem to be anything else in the area. I think it was the cinema newsreels that unsettled me because it made me think of my brothers and Don enduring dangers and hardships of wartime whilst I was in a safe and secure area and not really feeling the effects of the war. Shortly after our chat, Gillian arrived in her little red MG sports car and handed me a telegram. I don't know how she managed to arrange it but the telegram instructed me to report to London for a course in Code and Cipher at the School of Military Intelligence within the next few days. I was overjoyed because I felt I really would be in the thick of things in London. However my parents and friends thought I was crazy, exchanging a 'cushy' job for wartime London.

CHAPTER 13

London Calling!

THE FIRST THING I did when I arrived in London (the first visit of my life) was to confuse the taxi-driver with my Highland pronunciation of Cadogan Gardens. He asked me to repeat it and then corrected me; "It's not *Cado*gan, it's Ca*duggan* Gardens" he said kindly. That was my first introduction to a Cockney accent. When I had checked in, I was surprised to be informed that I was not going to a Code and Cipher school after all, but was to start work immediately at War Office Main Building in Whitehall. Up to that point my mother had always wakened me for work in the mornings and my first fear was that I would sleep in. However one of my room-mates had an alarm clock which played the tune 'Rose Marie, I love you' and I was thankful to waken at the right time that first morning and never again worried about oversleeping.

When I reported with one of the other girls to War Office, I was told that I would be instructed as I went along in encoding, decoding, enciphering and deciphering (code and cipher being two different things). If at the end of three months my work was found to be efficient, I would be promoted to Warrant Officer and put on the permanent staff. Our bosses were two civilian ex-naval officers from the Foreign Office and, while there was another Code and Cipher Branch attached to the army, we dealt more with political traffic in connection with MI6. We weren't informed of this officially but we gleaned as much from the nature of the messages we were dealing with. Our branch was known as C6. Whereas other ATS were allowed to wear London District (or Highland District) identification flashes, our branch were not allowed to wear such identification on our uniforms. However I discretely used my Cameron Highlander collar-dog as a tiepin and I wore my Cameron tartan skirt off duty. I don't think that did any harm, as any enemy agent who saw me would know that the Camerons were stationed in Inverness and that anyone wearing their tartan was probably just on leave in London.

I'll always be grateful to Gillian Mitford for arranging things for me and although at first everything was confusing, I soon grew used to the work. Our rooms (I think number 40 and 36) were situated deep down in the bowels of War Office and were reached either by a lift or by descending three flights of stairs. The rooms were air-conditioned and lit by strip-lighting. Sometimes on night duty, I used to think that the whine of the air conditioning sounded like the bagpipes and I would have a bout of the '*ciannalas*' (homesickness).

By the time the three months were up I was promoted to Warrant Officer. I made many friends and we went regularly to the ballet, the cinema and the theatre. On my 72-hours off after a spell of night duty I used to go down to Stowemarket in Suffolk, where my brother Kenny and his wife, Louie, were living.

Most of the girls were English but there were also few Scots and sometimes I went to the Scots Club in Fetter Lane or at Grosvenor House, Park Lane where we could meet with old friends who might be visiting London. We occupied several houses in Chelsea and our Mess was at 25 Draycott Place (which subsequently became a hotel and became notorious some years ago during the Jeremy Thorpe MP scandal). I managed to get a move from Cadogan Gardens to Draycott Place so that I wouldn't have to walk along the street for meals and I shared a room with two English girls – Joan and Jeanne. Our beds were just like ancient truckle beds with no springs, just solid wood as if carved out of a tree trunk with a dip in the middle. On top of this were three 'biscuits', which were square palliasses of straw. The first night I couldn't sleep as I felt the bed was uncomfortable but, after that, I slept like a log, even through the air raids!

A few nights after I arrived, there was an air raid and I, being Orderly Officer for the night, got up, went downstairs and tried to find the stirrup pump which I had no idea how to use but knew should be used to extinguish incendiary bombs. I found it down in the basement. As we had no air-raid shelter we were supposed to go down to the basement in the event of an air raid. Eventually, as nobody else in the house bothered to come downstairs, I went back to bed and that became the pattern from then onwards.

We were paid by the ATS Administrative Officers in their office in Chelsea but they had nothing to do with our working life and never came to War Office. There was a strange way of paying us; we got our flat pay according to our rank and then we got trade pay as Code and Cipher Operators. Over and above this, we got ten pence per day for each day we actually went to work at War Office, which meant that we didn't get War Office pay if we had a day off or during holidays. It seemed peculiar to us, but perhaps it was reckoned to be a sort of 'danger money'.

We hadn't much pay anyway (I think it was only around the equivalent of £3.50) but we didn't need much as we had our uniforms supplied, together with free food, laundry and the services of orderlies. I remember my orderly, Joy Matthews from Cromer, with a strong Norfolk accent, who was lovely and always had a bath running and a hot water bottle in the bed when I came off night duty. In peacetime Joy had been on the domestic staff of one of the other girls in War Office.

My colleagues were a motley crew but we all worked well together. The one who encouraged me most while on my probationary period was 'Bunny' Lisle who was married to an Irish Lord but she never used her title and we were all fond of her.

What surprised me was how little about Scotland some of the English girls appeared to know and that they considered the Highlands a remote outpost of the Empire. I would be asked, "What sort of lighting do you have in Inverness? Are the streets all cobbled?" This amused me because on visits to some of their homes in other parts of the country, I discovered that, in spite of the evidence of more wealthy parents, some of their houses were not so modern and the local facilities not as good as in Inverness. Sometimes the London girls were equally clueless about London; during the air raids, if the buses and tubes were out of action, they had no idea how to get about and I sometimes had the job of leading the way home. We used to go by tube from Sloane Square station to Westminster but on a good day we would walk through St James's Park and feed the ducks and then through Horse Guards Parade, which was almost opposite War Office. Going through the park it was hard to dodge the 'brass hats' (Staff Officers with gold braid and red bands on their hats and uniforms), who seemed to delight making us girls throw up our hands in the obligatory salute! During the latter days of the war we sometimes saw Princess Elizabeth (the Queen) going back to the Palace in her ATS uniform in her sleek chauffeur-driven limousine while we were on 'Shanks's pony'. However we all admired the royal family who were constantly seen around London during the darkest days of the war. I also grew to admire the London Cockneys for their great sense of humour and the way Hitler couldn't dampen their spirits. At first I was fascinated by the Cockney accent, as I had never heard a real live Cockney speak before. In pre-war days, we didn't meet Cockneys in the Highlands as the great tourist boom only started after the Second World War. We had heard them on the films of course but the only English accents we were used to were those of the 'huntin', shootin', fishin'' fraternity who came up for the shooting season and the Highland Games and balls.

When the raids were really bad the Londoners would perhaps leave for a while but they soon longed for home and came back again. We had a 'Mrs Mop' who cleaned our offices and saw that all our so-called 'secret waste' was sent for special disposal but, as the office was never empty, the work being done on shifts, she had difficulty when washing the floors. Although she had been bombed out of her home several times, she refused to leave London, as she put it, "… not for all the tea in China". I asked her once if she enjoyed her work and she told me that she did but that some of the girls were "awful snobs". I didn't really agree with her but asked which ones she particularly disliked. She mentioned one girl whom I thought quite nice but she was rather a well-built girl and had the habit of charging about and speaking in an affected voice as if she had a bad smell under her nose. 'Mrs Mop' went on to say to me, "I get my own back on her, though." When I asked her how she did this, she replied, "When I'm washing the floor and she is passing, I splash her legs with dirty water". I roared at this but kept the secret to myself and was glad my legs were never splashed.

Everything was rationed in those days and, when our sweet ration was consumed, we used to buy punnets of cherries from the barrow-boys. We weren't allowed to wear 'civvies' and so couldn't spend much on clothing but some of the London shops got round the question of clothing coupons by selling several yards of cloth, sewn up on three sides and described as mattress covers which were bought off coupons and easily available. I made several summer dresses out of Liberty fabric mattress covers and a tweed pinafore out of another. Even make-up and soap were scarce and it was quite usual for us to queue at Yardley's Bond Street salon for a bar of soap. We had to queue for everything, even for tickets for the ballet. We would go to the box-office in the morning and get a collapsible wooden stool (like a fishing stool) which we got for sixpence hire and we sat on it while we queued for tickets. Then in the evenings we would crowd into the 'Gods' to watch Margot Fontaine and Robert Helpmann dancing, or perhaps it would be opera or the Proms. Once I heard Dame Myra Hess playing the piano at a lunchtime concert at the National Gallery and that killed stone dead my ambition to be a concert pianist, as I knew I could never reach such dizzy heights.

'Lord Haw Haw' (William Joyce) who used to beam German propaganda over the airwaves would make one think that London life was all one of frugality and starvation of body and soul but this wasn't so. Life went on as usual and we always rushed to read the critic James Agate's column to see which show we would attend. He was our favourite critic and we went by his recommendation to the various shows. We saw lots of famous actors in the theatre during those years and Margot Fontaine was still dancing with Saddlers Wells Ballet (now the Royal Ballet, I think) long after the war. In fact, one period was spent co-partnering Donald MacLeary who was a chemist's son from Inverness. I wasn't keen on Grand Opera or Wagner but I enjoyed light opera and operettas. Due to working conditions in the underground office we liked to get out in the open air as much as possible and sometimes went into the country for a couple of days. We also had the chance of going to Chobham, where we stayed at a mansion house which was requisitioned for use as somewhere we could relax now and then, away from the office and London and where we were able to go cycling and walking in beautiful surroundings, so felt refreshed when back in the city.

The work became routine after a while. When I was home on leave, I would be asked questions like, "What will be the date of the 'Second Front'?" One neighbour asked me if I could find out when her husband, who had been posted to Trinidad in the West Indies, would be returning to the UK. Just because I was in the War Office, they thought I knew everything about future military strategy. At one time there was a big newspaper spread headed, 'The Girls who can keep Secrets', with interviews with some of the girls we knew who worked in the Code and Cipher Branch attached to the Army in War Office; but nothing was said about us, 'the Belles of C6 Tels', as we called ourselves. It appeared that C6 was non-existent as far as the public were concerned but we liked it that way.

There was a certain thrill about being at the centre of things in London at that time, rather reminding me of Wordsworth's lines about the French Revolution, '… Bliss was it in that dawn to be alive, but to be young was very Heaven'. Everything seemed so intense when I wrote the following lines but it is very difficult now to recapture the feeling of waiting for one's last moment to come.

London's Burning

Bofors* are trundled down the street.
Next door, the sound of marching feet.
(Poor Yanks! It is their first night here –
They'll find war's not all skittles and beer!).

---

* Bofors – mobile anti-aircraft guns trundled through the streets during an air-raid.

I hear them running helter-skelter
Out the door to air-raid shelter,
While I lie trembling here in bed
And watch the 'dog-fights' overhead.

The birds still sing and the flowers bloom
But Man's eyes are closed to beauty
And Man lust for Man's blood and calls
This murderous instinct 'duty'.
"I say, there, Joan, are you sleeping?"
"No, but I can hear Jeanne weeping".
"Jeanne, go back to golden slumbers.
You know OUR BOMB will have OUR NUMBERS".

I wonder if that Hun up there
Is having fun or is aware,
In spite of all of Hitler's might,
We're in the fight for God and Right.
Perhaps he feels a bit like me …
Extremely near eternity;
Or does he long for his true love
Whom MINE may be bombing from above?

"Bring out your dead", they used to say.
(Our dead are with us, night and day);
But life and death go hand-in-hand
And I am young – and life is grand.
London's burning, left and right
But Jerry has been put to flight.
Not to worry; soon be day …
And lots of time for work and play.

There wasn't much room for personal belongings but we tried to brighten up our rooms. While the servicemen had their pin-ups of Betty Grable, and so on, some of the girls had photographs of their family and sometimes photographs of film stars pinned up behind their beds. At first I shared a room with two friends but, when one was posted away (much to our regret as we all got on so well together and we are still in touch), we could spread out a little. My pin-up was a different kettle of fish from most of the girls. I had a huge newspaper spread of Sir Fitzroy MacLean, walking along a road, resplendent in his Cameron Highlander kilt and balmoral with the royal blue hackle behind his cap badge (the Black Watch had a red hackle). He had been parachuted into Yugoslavia, working for most of the war with General Tito and his partisans and later became our man in Moscow, with a great knowledge of Russia and Communism. I had never met Sir Fitzroy but I thought he epitomised the type of Highlander who had fought in the 'Forty-five' (1745) Jacobite Rebellion with 'Bonnie Prince Charlie' (Charles Edward Stewart, the Young Pretender).

I was really fortunate in my roommates but we were sensible enough not to live in each other's pockets. We had other friends with different interests; and we weren't always on the same shift at the office. However, Joan M. and Jeanne were both keen on ballet and the theatre, whereas some of my other friends weren't. All my friends seemed to be bookworms like myself and we joined the Reprint Society Book Club (now World Books, I think). We would discuss the various books and then search the barrow-boys' piles of books or Foyle's shop in Charing Cross Road, where I picked up some fine second-hand books which I still have in my bookcase. Another pastime we had was sewing 'Penelope' tapestry, which didn't cost anything like it does to-day. It helped to pass the time in the Mess and steady our fingers during air raids. My 'masterpiece' was a petit-point embroidered silk picture of an eighteenth century drawing room with a woman playing a spinet and a man leaning over the instrument and gazing into her eyes. I admit it took me about a year to complete but it hangs in my living-room to-day and, at a distance, looks like a painting. I never had the time or the patience to do another one although I've often searched for a companion piece which I would probably have tried to complete.

Sometimes we would wander up and down the King's Road nearby and go into the numerous antique shops there. I much admired some pieces of china and I promised myself I would buy two of the articles

I had seen in a window there. One was an old-fashioned brass warming-pan and the other was a china ornament depicting an old-fashioned high bed with one person lying it and another two getting in on either side, with a caption below reading, 'Last in bed to put out the light'. This because it had been the nightly call at home in Inverness and Joan, Jeanne and I had adopted it as we struggled to reach our beds first. By the time I was preparing to go home, this ornament had vanished and I had to settle for a little bud vase with a minute raised bunch of forget-me-nots up and down the stem, in a *capodimonte* style. As for the warming-pan, once the Americans came over the prices leapt up and anyway, I had no room for it in my khaki grip by the time I had packed all my bits and pieces.

CHAPTER 14

Life in Whitehall

W E THOUGHT that working underground for long periods during those years would leave a mark on us after the war, but it had no effect as far as I was concerned. Sometimes we were given the opportunity to go up to the top of War Office building and undergo treatment with sun lamps and ultra violet rays; but we soon wearied of this and preferred the outdoor life in the park whenever we had the chance. We had the added bonus of a tennis court in Cadogan Gardens.

While on night duty, which was such a long spell, from 5 pm until 9 am next day, we were able to snatch one-and-a-half hours' sleep in the early hours in a room along the corridor where there were double bunks. I was fortunate enough never having to sleep in a bottom bunk, where a girl once said a rat had run over her. I think I would have died with fright as, every time I had to take my turn to make tea, I would throw the lid of the kettle into the washroom before I put on the light so that any rats there would hide before I came in. Of course we were so near the Thames that we had huge iron flood doors to keep out the water from the river but I daresay there were plenty of places where rats could get in. I'll never forget the martinets we called 'Aunties' who were in charge of the washrooms and toilets. They wouldn't allow us to comb hair over the washbasins and they were as keen as Sherlock Holmes in trying to detect whose strand of hair lay near the plughole in the washbasin. All the same, the lavatories were kept scrupulously clean.

One night when I was walking along the corridor to open the door of the bunkhouse and waken the half of the shift who were sleeping so that the rest of us could get our kip, I saw a man in pyjamas walking towards me with a towel over his arm. When I got level with him, I realised that it was the Prime Minister, Mr Churchill, who had walked along the underground passage from Downing Street. He would probably be over in connection with some urgent matter necessitating his sleeping at the War Office which happened quite often during wartime. As we passed, we each said, "Good evening," without a pause. That was the only time I saw him at very close quarters at War Office, however we often saw him in public, particularly when he was visiting the Liberal Club along the street. Although I frequently deciphered messages headed 'For Mr Churchill's Eyes Only' our messages were delivered by uniformed messengers, usually retired servicemen, not by us in person. We knew the bunk in which Mr Churchill regularly stayed during these emergencies and when passing, we were much amused to see Mr Churchill's own Ministerial chamber-pot or 'chanty' stored below his bunk-bed at War Office!

Sometimes, when there was a vacancy at OCTU (Officers' Training Unit), we would be asked if we wanted to apply but we decided to consider our options first. Two of the girls we knew had gone and, although they had come back to work at the jobs they did before, they had never got any promotion since and remained Subalterns (2nd Lieutenants, the lowest Commissioned Rank) for the rest of the war. There was no prospect in the office for further promotion, our bosses being two civilians; retired ex-Naval Officers from Foreign Office. It didn't follow that we would be posted back and we might have had to go out to a dreaded command post. In addition, by talking with those girls who did come back, we discovered that we would have gained very little financially by the transition, as the small increase in pay would be offset by the fact that we would have to buy our uniforms, employ a separate orderly (equivalent to a male Officer's 'batman') and pay hefty mess fees, whereas we shared an orderly, got our uniforms free and our mess bills were minimal. The officers couldn't patronise other ranks' clubs but had to pay quite big fees for officers' clubs. An additional disadvantage, as far as I was concerned, was that Don was in the ranks in the Air Force and had no intention of applying for a commission. In all, we worked out that we would be worse off all round and, as we were called 'Ma'am' by the other ranks in the same way as the women commissioned officers were, we decided we were quite happy to jog along as we were.

During the times when most of the children were evacuated from London, the teaching staff had no pupils to teach; but we were asked if we would help to keep some of the teachers in Battersea School (over the bridge from us in Chelsea) employed by attending some of their cookery classes on our days off. Some of us decided to do just that. I myself had no experience of cooking and my husband used to tease me that before I married him I couldn't boil an egg properly. He was probably right. The part of the school we attended was an annexe built like a house, with kitchen, dining room, bedroom, sitting-room and bathroom and we were really being taught cooking and 'housewifery'. There were three cookers, one of which was solid fuel and the others, gas and electricity.

We took it in turns to cook, serve meals and look after the 'house'. The housekeeping involved going shopping for food in the local shops and going to the local house furnishers with coupons to 'buy' furniture which was delivered to the house. What was there already was then uplifted and returned to the shop, say, once a month. The furniture was what was termed 'Utility', rather like G-plan, but inferior in quality. It looked pretty fragile, although more modern than the heavier furniture. We were also given the choice of changing the wallpaper and décor, but I was never very good at it or interested in that sort of work and, when my turn came, I left the wallpaper as it was. We got a very good training and it must have helped the Battersea girls prepare for life after leaving school. We were taught 'homely measures' which meant we didn't have to use scales when baking. One recipe I didn't take to was the teacher's recipe for porridge. She made it in a double saucepan, very thickly and then left it to set. Once it set, she told us to slice it and fry it, which made me utter the Invernessian exclamation of disgust, "gyaddies!"

The food in our Mess was quite good. We had breakfast, lunch and dinner. The dinner and lunch were full-course meals, as some of the girls going on night duty had their dinner at lunchtime. There always seemed to be plenty of lean meat, so much so that we sometimes wondered if it was horsemeat as there seemed to be so little fat on it. It may be hard to believe that we were allowed only one egg a month but this was a fact. We would look forward so much to our monthly egg, only to find, more often than not, that the orderlies had cooked it earlier and then left it on the hotplate in the Mess, with the result that it was like leather, whereas I always liked a soft egg. Tomatoes were also scarce but we grew some on the balcony outside the sitting-room in the Mess. There were lots of self-service restaurants where we could get snacks and there was no shortage of cream buns, although I expect the cream was 'ersatz'. There were lots of milkbars where we could buy milkshakes, yoghurt and hot waffles, dripping with syrup and, of course the usual sort of expensive restaurants in London. When we were on night duty at War Office we would either feed at the canteen in QMG (Quartermaster-General) House, which was reached through a labyrinth of tunnels under Whitehall or we could get a chit for an outside restaurant. We were rather fond of vegetarian food and went for lunch to a restaurant called 'The Vega' in Leicester Square, which sold only vegetarian food. I had previously thought of vegetarian food as being just cold salads but there was a variety of vegetarian dishes served there, along the lines of Dr Bircher Benner's sanitorium in Zurich. I bought a book written by Dr Benner full of his vegetarian recipes. My favourite lunch was vegetable soup followed by fresh red cabbage, stewed with onions and apples with a nut cutlet and the sweets were delicious. Muesli was billed as a dietetic dish and was served with fruit as a sweet which we enjoyed. Usually our chit wouldn't cover what we wanted to eat and we had to pay the difference.

When we were on night duty, from 5 pm to 9 am next morning, we either went to the canteen or to Lyons Corner House in the Strand, where we had arranged to have tables reserved for us. It always seemed to be full of young men in civilian clothes and, being at two to four o'clock in the morning, we wondered at this as they seemed to be moving from table to table. We were cordoned off in a different part of the restaurant and those young men were the only other patrons and so, being inquisitive, I asked the waiter one night who they were. When he answered that they were, "… pansies, picking up boy-friends". I must confess I didn't know what he meant, even although I was over twenty-one. I thought a 'pansy' was just a very feminine lad. Present-day teenagers would think we were naive but I think my generation was very innocent of the ways of the world. I don't think there are any corner houses left, but in those days during the day there was always a small orchestra playing for the tea dance and a lot of the shops had music in their restaurants. The only orchestra I found recently was the one in the Harrods restaurant.

We were told that we could wear our Cameron tartan skirts off-duty which we often did. On one occasion I was going down the escalator when a crowd of French matelots were ascending. I heard one of them shouting, "Ecossaise!" and all the matelots turned towards me. On another occasion, a troop of servicemen were marching down the centre of the road and caught sight of me. I heard the order, "Eyes right!" being shouted and all hands went up in salute which I had to return!

We loved going round the shops but because of coupons and shortage of cash we mostly indulged in window-shopping. We weren't so keen on the Oxford Street shops but we liked the Kensington shops of those days (Barkers, Pontings and Derry & Toms). We often shopped at Peter Jones, which was a large glass-fronted department store in Sloane Square and we loved Harrods, which was just a short walk along Sloane Street to Knightsbridge. When I married I got the loan of a friend's wedding dress to save coupons, and as a result, I was able to buy my going-away outfit from Harrods. My friend and room-mate Joan M. had an electric sewing-machine and ran up some beautifully hand-embroidered white *crepe-de-chine* material I bought in Liberty's for my nightdress.

Jeanne, my other room-mate was a Catholic and, sometimes coming off night duty, she would go to Westminster Cathedral and I would go along too. At other times she would get up at 7.30 am and go to Mass at the church round the corner. I wondered at this as our other friend on the opposite side of the landing was Catholic but didn't go to church. Joan M. was Church of England but used to come with me to the Pont Street Church of Scotland, which was bombed, after which services were held in the Hall of India (Jehanger Hall) next to the Royal School of Needlework in Kensington. There was a Scottish church at Covent Garden called Crown Court Church where there was a Gaelic Service once a month and I always made a point of going to it when I could, although I didn't really understand a lot of what was said. Church Gaelic is similar to English in the Bible, in that it is phrased in old-fashioned language and is difficult for a non-native Gaelic speaker to grasp; but I could close my eyes during the service and listen to the Gaelic psalm-singing and feel near 'my ain folk'.

CHAPTER 15

A Wartime Wedding

Don and I had become engaged on New Year's Day 1939 and my original resolution of not marrying until the age of thirty flew out of the window. We had planned to marry in 1940, as Don had set up in business as a painter/decorator on his own account on the Isle of Skye to be nearer the mainland and where we had spent some holidays. Sometimes I would take a daily excursion ticket on the train for Kyle and cross the ferry at Kyleakin where Don would be waiting for me to spend a day together. When war broke out we decided not to marry until the war was over but, as time went on and it looked as if the war would never be over, we decided to marry whenever we could get a furlough together because our meetings had become few and far between.

During the war most of the Highlands and Islands were designated a 'protected area' and we needed to apply for special identify cards to carry when we returned home on leave. Every time we settled on a wedding date, it had to be changed because of what was called 'the exigencies of the service', i.e. neither of us could get leave at the same time. At last we settled on 15th October, 1943. We thought we would have to start planning all over again when Don's stepmother died suddenly on 13th October in Lewis. We were in a quandary about whether Don could go to the funeral but thought it was 'now or never' for our wedding, even although we both loved his stepmother, Kirsty Lizzie, who had brought him up after his mother died. None of Don's people were able to come to the wedding and none of my brothers came except Alex, who had been wounded with the 51st Highland Division in France and had been invalided out of the Army so was back in his civilian job. Because of rationing we were only allowed thirty people at the reception and those consisted mostly of family friends, most of our friends serving at the time. I don't remember much about the day except that the weather was dull and the photographs were taken in a studio. I do remember that my dad, in his speech, described Don as being 'of very good stock' and I remember my friend Margaret, from Highland District days playing the Wedding March; another friend Peggy sang in French, *'J'attendrai'* ('I will be waiting'); my blind cousin Peggy sang *'Thug mi mo Lamh d'on Eilaneach'* ('I gave my Love to an Islander') and Allan, the husband of Cathie, who had given me the loan of her wedding dress, sang in Gaelic *'Fagail Leodhais'* ('Leaving Lewis'). Whenever I hear any of those songs being played on the radio I am transported back to that happy day.

The wedding-dress was of white satin, with leg o' mutton sleeves and a long trailing veil. My bouquet was a shower of deep red roses and I had sent to my Uncle John in Lewis for some wild white heather from the Gravir hills, which I held in my bouquet, fastened with the silk Cameron tartan ribbon from my father's bagpipes. My bridesmaids were my sister Marie and chum Ruth who looked gorgeous in pink taffeta dresses, with light blue organdie overskirts cut away at the waist and bouquets of pink and blue anemones. Their rosette headdresses and their dresses were designed and made by another friend Marion, from Highland District days. Alex was the best man and my sister Marion's kilted little boy John was page. We could only have a short honeymoon and had to leave on the 4 pm train south to Pitlochry. We spent a couple of days there and then Don had to go back to Wig Bay, near Stranraer where he was stationed, working with Sunderland Flying Boats. As I had a longer furlough, I managed to stay in Stranraer with Don for another few days before returning to War Office.

We were planning another leave together when, out of the blue, Don got a posting to Ireland at Castle Archdale, County Fermanagh, near the border with Eire. Of course, I couldn't quit the services until war was over so couldn't go over with him. It was around this time that we were told we were not allowed to travel more than 25 miles out of London due to the imminent threat of invasion. I received a letter, addressed to me personally at my billet, instructing me to take a little attaché case with 'necessities' to War Office, in case of London being under siege; our work would have to go on regardless. Don and I kept in touch and I remember writing him every day during the war but I wonder now what I had to say to fill two or three pages. It would probably have been plans for our future life together.

CHAPTER 16

Hair Raising at the Salon

O NCE the Americans came into the war, they swept many girls off their feet, according to the media, being 'overpaid, oversexed and over here'. I told the girls to be careful in case they ended up marrying hobos and going back to America to live in a shack with them!

We became quite friendly with some Americans who were stationed in the house next door, as they used to invite us into their Mess to see American films which hadn't been generally released in Britain and we in turn invited them into our Mess on our 'open nights'. They were a branch of the American Army Air Corps and their job was to fit together for intelligence purposes, the 'mosaics' (the photographs their reconnaissance planes took when over the continent). Sometimes they were very noisy, sitting out on their balconies, playing guitars and singing loudly when our girls were trying to sleep during the day, after a night-shift. It bothered some of the girls but it didn't bother me as I found I could sleep anywhere, after the first experience of sleeping in my 'dug-out canoe' of a bed. Someone complained about the noise and it stopped for a while but it soon started off again and I expect it could be annoying when they came out on their balcony to sit on a good day. Whenever there was an air raid alarm we could hear the Americans rushing downstairs in their heavy boots and forming outside ready to go to the nearest air-raid shelter. Towards the end of the war, we were very sorry when eighty of them (including some in other houses nearby) were killed one morning while boarding military wagons down the street. That was one bomb that wakened me out of my sleep.

Whenever anyone from Inverness came down to London, I would be asked out for a meal and the theatre and I remember doing several tours of the city with servicemen who I knew from back home. Some of them were French Canadians and some were Norwegians who had been stationed near Inverness and we got to know them through the dances each held at their Mess. I didn't keep in touch with them but there was always a wonderful spirit of camaraderie between the Forces in those days and, whenever they were coming down to London, they would ask for my address so that they would have a companion to show them round. I remember one of the French Canadians making a beeline out of St Martins-in-the-Fields Church when I was showing him around and I wondered why. He said, "This isn't a Catholic Church". I asked how he knew, and he answered, "Because there's no incense." So I brought him to Westminster Cathedral and we went right up to the top of the tower, which had a gorgeous view of the city. Sometimes I would be asked to make up a four by some of my friends and I ate at Claridges, the Ritz and some of the other classy places during the war. I didn't think much of the Ritz then, as it seemed quite rundown at that time but I liked Claridges. If we made a *faux pas* at table at home my mum used to say, "We couldn't take you to the Ritz," so it was a comedown to see the Ritz so shabby. Sometimes my chum Rene's sister-in-law, who was a First Aid Nursing Yeomanry driver stationed in Southampton, came up to London and we would have a night out at Park Lane Hotel with her fiancé (a Canadian) and one of his friends.

We used to get complimentary tickets to some of the theatre shows and that saved quite a bit. Sometimes, coming back from lunching at the 'Vega' in Leicester Square, we would have to pass a long queue of servicemen waiting to go into Whitehall Theatre to see the striptease artiste Phyllis Dixey and we would contrive to look the other way, wondering what prompted those men to go to a striptease show in the middle of the day!

One commodity which wasn't rationed was hairdressing and we used to patronise the 'court hairdressers' of the day, Henri and Vasco.

Joan M. liked Henri's salon but I preferred Vasco and remember getting a 'Vasco bubble' which was a short, brushed back loose curly style but not too severe. We weren't allowed to wear hairstyles where the hair touched the top of our collar – so we couldn't have long, flowing hairstyles. We could sometimes let our hair grow and put it up in a roll, but that was difficult to keep tidy.

One afternoon my friend Joan M. (I had another friend Joan D.) and I went to Simpson's, Piccadilly, who had opened a new hairdressing salon, on the open-plan system instead of the usual individual cubicle style. We sat side-by-side to have our hair done. When an assistant told us that they had installed a new system of scalp vibration which was supposed to do wonders to the hair, we opted for the treatment, having nothing more glamorous to spend our money on at the time. We were each wired up to a cabinet like the plug in an old-fashioned telephone exchange and they were secured to our head with some sort of curler. All was going well, when we heard a 'Doodlebug' (V1 Rocket) whirr-whirr-whirring in the distance. The two assistants gave high-pitched screams and ran downstairs, leaving us upstairs unable to move, as we were tied to our 'telephone' cabinet. We couldn't do anything but stay where we were and, when the noise of the 'Doodlebug' seemed to stop just overhead, we knew it would fall straight down and explode. All I could say was, "Although I expected to be bombed in London one day, I never thought that I might be scalped". Fortunately, the 'Doodlebug' exploded elsewhere and the assistants returned sheepishly to free us from the contraption ... and never again did we opt for that sort of hair-raising hairdressing!

We thought the worst raids were the V1 raids and I remember the horror of the first one. I was on day duty at the time but we were very puzzled as, during the previous night, the sirens kept going on and off all night. There were countless bumps and we couldn't understand why because usually Jerry went off home when daylight came. Going on duty next morning we asked the night shift why the alert was still going on and we were told that the Germans were sending over what they called 'pilotless planes' and that this must be the secret weapon we had heard so much about in our messages. In an ordinary air-raid, one sees the planes coming over and we used to watch the dogfights in the sky and the bombs dropping; but, with the 'Doodlebugs', one could hear the drone of its engine coming in fits and starts nearer and nearer and we knew that when the drone stopped, it would fall down and explode. Once we heard the explosion and thought we were safe, we would hear another V1 coming in the distance as they used to come over in groups of five. It was said that they were fired in a haphazard manner and that the Germans weren't sure where they would fall but I don't believe this as several of the V1s and V2s fell quite near us; one of each falling on Chelsea Barracks. The V2s were more sophisticated but not as frightening as they were said to travel faster than sound so that, when we saw the light of the explosion, we knew we were safe. It was the case that the ordinary air-raid wasn't so psychologically nerve-wracking as the 'Doodlebugs'. Some girls had to be posted away from London owing to their nervous state. It was then decided that a direct hit on our houses, which were all around Cadogan Gardens in Chelsea, would be a setback for the cipher work at War Office so if anyone had relatives in London and wanted to live out, they could do so, as that would disperse the staff all over London. Quite a few of the girls decided to take advantage of this and some gave the excuse of going to stay with 'my Auntie's family', or some such relative, whereas, in reality it might be an American serviceman!

We hadn't enough room to store anything other than our uniforms and personal effects but a few of us decided that we would set about getting a flat to rent so that we could bring down some civilian clothes for special outings. We weren't supposed to wear civvies in wartime but I don't think we did much harm in breaking this rule. We managed to get a one-roomed flat in Cheyne Walk nearby where we occasionally went to change. One of my friends was a girl from Southern Ireland and if she had worn uniform when going on leave to Eire, she would have been interned, so she used to leave her uniform in the flat when she went home. I suppose a similar flat in Cheyne Walk today would cost the earth but we paid, among six of us, six shillings a week all in. Of course I don't remember any of us staying overnight; I certainly didn't but, later on in the war, when one of the other girls married a

South African serviceman and they couldn't find anywhere to stay, we thought it might help them along until something else turned up and we gave the flat to them.

As well as my friend from Southern Ireland, we had other nationalities in our branch at War Office – one from Belgium, South Africa and an Indian Jewess. She wouldn't eat anything but kosher meat and rarely ate in the mess. Everybody seemed to dislike this Indian girl and I wondered why. My brother Angus, who spent so much time in the Army in India in peace and wartime, told me that perhaps the girl was a Parsee rather than a Jewess but I was never very sure of this. In the Highlands and, especially in the Islands, there is a sort of classlessness, without taking much note of the status of the person. My Irish friend had an upper-class English accent as she had been educated at a convent in England, but she could relapse into an Irish brogue whenever she was annoyed about the English, when she miscalled them and repeatedly told me, "My mother fought in the revolution and slept in a barn for three nights when she was on the run from the English". I expect she was referring to the Easter Rising in 1916. At any rate, that same mother refused to have her daughter home when she was discharged from the ATS under 'Para ll' which related to the birth of a child; but she was taken under the wing of one of the London girl's mothers until she got settled elsewhere, as the baby was put up for adoption. I lost touch with this dear friend but another friend told me that all went well for her thereafter and she became an air hostess and got married. She had turned down a fine young man who was the son of a peer and who was the host at our table at Claridges. I couldn't really understand her, as she wouldn't go to any of the functions in the Mess or the Office and had no interest except in this fellow she had met while working out at a Command post. The man in question was from the home town of Joan M. who knew him quite well and told me that, although he was an officer, he had just been employed as a clerk in a lawyer's office and she couldn't see how he could afford a divorce and keep up his family of three children.

Some of the girls looked well in their uniforms and some looked downright dowdy. One of my friends, who shared the Cheyne Walk apartment, was untidy in her uniform and yet, in her tweed suits she looked classy. She had worked in the film industry in Wardour Street in pre-war days and knew quite a lot of people in the theatre and film. I seem to have a vague memory of her introducing me to Jack Buchanan, the musical star and, another time, we shared a table in the Vega with Alasdair Sim and his son. I laughed when this friend told me she had been invited up to a certain Colonel's estate near Inverness and asked me if I knew him as she was going to a house-party there. She had a lovely personality and had an 'air' about her when she dressed up and she was so full of fun. I was most amused about this Colonel she mentioned but said that I didn't know him personally, I just knew of him. Indeed I had heard quite a lot about his 'nude parties' before the war, if this were to be believed! When my friend returned, I asked her about how she got on and she said she had enjoyed her time up north and that the scenery was beautiful. I never asked or found out if there had been any nude parties.

I remembered how amused we were when we were told that there would be black Americans coming to billets somewhere off Sloane Street and that we should be careful not to refer to them as 'black'. I was once going round in circles between Sloane Square tube station and Draycott Place in a deep pea-soup fog and a black soldier and his girlfriend came along, so we joined up to find our way home.

I expect there were crimes on the streets of London during the war but, somehow or other, we weren't aware of it and I thought nothing of walking home alone in the blackout, perhaps all along Piccadilly, Knightsbridge or from Victoria, when the buses and tubes weren't running. Our one thought was to get to work in time to relieve the other shift or else get home before dawn! There were some family friends in London whom I visited now and then; particularly some Hebridean girls in Earls Court and Baker Street who were working as nurses in London. I sometimes stayed for a night or two with friends who lived in one of the huge mansions in Brook Street and, although this would sometimes intrigue my ATS friends, I didn't tell them that these friends didn't own the house but were caretakers for a titled lord whose family had fled London because of the air-raids. I sometimes visited the parents of one of my ex-colleagues from Highland area days. He was a trainee surveyor in civilian life and was in the Royal Engineers and had made me promise to visit his folks in Enfield once I settled in London. I sometimes visited them and I remember once there was great excitement, when one of his friends arrived at his parents' house with a tape-recorder to record a message from all of us before it was posted to India, where he had gone from Highland area. He was one of the pals who used to bring us chips when we were working late at Highland district where we were all part of 'the crowd'. I had met many pals while in the Army and they were all fine fellows and I sometimes wonder if they survived the war. So many of my school classmates were killed in the war that I was surprised when a former classmate told me that Alasdair MacLean, the novelist of *Guns of Navarone* fame, had been one of our classmates at school.

During my time in London, I visited most of the places of interest there; Windsor, Ascot, Epsom, Hampton Court and all the other well-known sites. I loved the museums and art galleries and would spend hours there. Later in life I became a member of the National Art Collection Fund, which was established to try to prevent works of art being bought and shipped abroad. The Fund raised quite a lot of money in those days and, among other purchases, managed to prevent a Canaletto going to America. Inverness museum was presented with a pair of Jacobite pistols which the fund had rescued. On the occasion of the seventy-fifth anniversary of the fund, there was a ballot for a visit to Buckingham Palace to tour all the works of art there that the general public weren't normally allowed to see (although they could visit the 'Queen's Gallery' adjacent to the Palace). I was lucky to get a place and enjoyed seeing all the special rooms in the Palace such as the throne room and the room where George V, VI and our Queen made their Christmas speeches. The man who conducted us round the Palace was, at that time, the Keeper of the Queen's Art Treasures; the infamous Sir Anthony Blunt, who soon afterwards lost his title and everything else after he was exposed as a Soviet spy.

Since leaving London in 1945, I've just passed through it *en route* to the continent or when visiting my brother Angus in Dorset, but a few years ago, I accompanied one of my daughters on a tour of London. I was saddened at the conglomeration of buildings around St Paul's Cathedral and when I came home I heard the Prince of Wales saying the same thing on TV. It reminded me of the shoots of London pride I used to see popping up among the ruins in that area after the Germans had left almost nothing but St Paul's standing in glorious isolation.

Although I was terrified of air raids and although we had permission to use the air raid shelter below the Peter Jones store, we continued to remain in our beds at the top of the house. Our chant became, 'our bombs will have our numbers' and I had the impudence to think that, because I prayed to God, He would see to it that nothing would happen to me! We didn't see the point of having to get up in the middle of the night and dress to walk a couple of hundred yards to an air raid shelter. Incidentally, Peter Jones's store remained standing in spite of it having a large glass front and, even when a land-mine landed nearby and windows were broken on the King's Road, Peter Jones's store windows remained intact. Bomb blast has a strange effect and seems to travel in a sort of finger pattern. One morning when we were having breakfast in the Mess, we heard an awful blast and were astounded to see the two large plate-glass windows in the Mess being blown inside just like a glass-blower effect and then they went back to their original position, without a pane of glass being broken. That was something I never saw in my life again. I don't really think we considered ourselves brave but we became fatalistic. I remember that sometimes during a bad raid I would get up from bed and put on my steel helmet and then jump back into bed again as I had a phobia about being blinded by shrapnel. I must have looked a strange sight, lying in bed in my pyjamas with my tin hat on!

We were very fortunate in that none of our houses were bombed, although I came home one night to see a nearby block of modern flats (I think they were called 'Nell Gwynn Mansions') burning fiercely. During the Doodlebug bombings we could hear mobile Bofor guns being trundled around the streets, reminding me of the days of the plague, when the shout went up, "Bring out your dead". There was a marvellous spirit of camaraderie and humour in the air and people cheered madly when the King and Queen or Mr Churchill appeared among the ruins of bombed buildings.

When the weather was good we would sometimes sunbathe on the roof of our house, to which we gained access through a trapdoor with an attached ladder. As the roof was flat, we got various lectures about what to do if a German parachutist landed. We were told that we must give him nothing; no food or information. We thought this absolutely stupid, as he would probably shoot us in any case and then go down to the basement for food unhindered.

The tubes, buses and billboards were covered with stickers sporting slogans such as, 'Billy Brown of London Town says "Coughs and sneezes spread diseases"; "Trap your germs in your handkerchiefs"; "Careless talk costs lives" or "Even walls have ears"'. In fact, 'Billy Brown of London Town' was constantly warning us about something! Like most young folk, we enjoyed a good feed and joined several clubs where we would get a meal and there were one or two Greek restaurants in Sloane Square which were quite reasonable. One evening Joan M. and three of our friends from the north of England decided that chips in a restaurant weren't half as tasty as chips in a newspaper from a chip shop so we decided to scour the area for one. We knew we wouldn't find one going down Sloane Street to the Knightsbridge area; so we walked up the King's Road, asking folk on our way where we could find a chip shop. We had walked miles up the Fulham Road when we came to a place called 'World's End' and that was where we got our chips in a newspaper. On the return journey we walked down the street guzzling our chips out of a newspaper and the meal was all we had hoped for.

There was a pub near Chelsea Barracks that some of our friends went to. I had never been in a pub before, although we sometimes went to a licensed restaurant cum-cocktail bar for a meal. There was a famous pianist (or so we were told) who used to play in one of those establishments. We didn't know his full name or anything about him except that he was a talented pianist. We just knew he was called Paul and later on in life I sometimes came across a reference to him as, 'Paul of Chelsea'. One of my father's friends from Inverness had bought a pub next to Chelsea Barracks and my dad told me to call on this Army pal of his but somehow or other I never got round to it. The few girls who went there said it was usually full of Chelsea Pensioners. Halfway up the King's Road there was a large house standing on its own with steps leading up to it and as it seemed so isolated from other buildings it looked rather sinister. It was called 'The Pheasantry' and we used to make up all manner of stories about what went on there. It may have been a most respectable club, but we sometimes regaled some of our more gullible friends with descriptions of visits we had made there; but quite frankly, none of us would have had the nerve to go near the front door.

There was a call for girls to fill three vacancies with the British Military Mission in Washington and three girls whom I knew put forward their names. None of my friends volunteered; although the idea of going to Washington seemed quite exciting there was a down side to the posting. The tour of duty was only for eighteen months after which those returning to the UK would be posted out to a Command post and couldn't come back to War Office. Another disadvantage was that, before going to Washington, one had to step down in rank from Warrant Officer to Sergeant (two ranks below) as there was no establishment for Warrant Officers in Washington. If this had happened to me, coming from an Army background, my folks and friends back home would think that I had committed an awful crime and been demoted as a punishment. The biggest deterrent to my going to America was that my husband was stationed in Europe at that time and I was afraid something might happen to him and I would be too far away.

The girls who went to Washington got quite a lot of publicity in America and our three friends graced the front page of the 'Picture Post', walking down the steps of the White House in one edition of the magazine. A bonus, as far as they were concerned, was that they were allowed to wear civvies and had servants instead of orderlies to wait upon them. I'm afraid that, after their eighteen-month assignment, they were posted elsewhere and we lost touch with them.

Although we didn't have to pay for our uniforms, as Warrant Officers we could have purchased uniforms of finer material similar to those the officers wore. However we were quite content to wear the coarser uniform issue, except that we thought khaki of any quality was a horrible colour; and it amuses me today to see how fashionable it has become. In fact, we were issued with khaki 'overalls' which I never had occasion to wear and which were very similar to today's safari suits. We had to wear light brown flat laced walking shoes unlike the court shoes worn by the present day Women's Royal Army Corps. We had lisle khaki stockings; so, to make us look that little bit smarter, we bought Kaysor-Bondor silk khaki stockings and went along to Moss Bros to buy braid ties instead of the cotton type issue, which always seemed to go out of shape. We bought 'cheesecutter' hats of stiffer material than the issue and bronze cap badges which we wouldn't have to polish like the brass ones. We had also our forage caps with coloured braiding round the top which we sometimes wore off duty. We were issued with small khaki shoulder bags, rather like the Burberry type, which were quite smart. I sewed a two-inch shoulder flash of the Highland Division on my bag which was quite unorthodox but wouldn't have helped an enemy agent in any way. He or she would probably have known that, at that time, the original 51st Highland Division were languishing in prison camps in Germany and Silesia and the newly constituted 51st was stationed in the Middle East.

We still went on singing during the war, encouraged by Vera Lynn and the others who sang those nostalgic songs like, 'The White Cliffs of Dover' and 'We'll Meet Again'. Some of the songs we sang then have a new lease of life today, such as, 'As Time Goes by' and 'Begin the Beguine'. We danced to the Big Bands and Glenn Miller's music was favourite with us. We danced at Hammersmith Palais where there was a large revolving stage with a band on each side, which took turns to play. One band was the famous all-girl Ivy Benson Band and they were every bit as good as the other, which I think was Lou Prager's. We watched the Yanks doing jitterbugging and jiving and they could fairly swing their partners around but when it came to real ballroom dancing, they smooched around at walking pace, even for a quickstep.

We preferred straight theatre but for a laugh we also used to enjoy the Aldwych Farces with Tom Walls, Robertson Hare and Ralph Lynn, which involved lots of doors opening and closing and people rushing in and out. We weren't so keen on the music halls but I remember once going to Victoria Palace to hear Richard Tauber singing. We thought it sad that this once great tenor had deteriorated to the level of singing in a variety theatre. I think, for a while, he conducted an orchestra at the end of his singing career. I was fortunate to get an album of cassettes from my daughter for a recent birthday and it contains most of the 'hit' songs of our youth sung by Tauber: 'One Day When we were Young', 'In the Still of the Night', 'Night and Day', 'Schubert's Serenade' and 'We'll Gather Lilacs'. I'm so glad that compact discs are being made of Tauber's singing which will introduce him to a wider audience. Of course we couldn't miss getting caught up in the Cockney culture and danced the 'Lambeth Walk' and 'Underneath the Spreading Chestnut Tree' and sang songs like 'Me and my Girl' and 'You are my Sunshine'.

Being based in Whitehall was also very handy for visiting the House of Commons and listening to some of the debates. Following these debates, as a souvenir I usually retained the copy of the 'Notices of Motions and Orders of the Day' pamphlet which are now fascinating to look back on. There were debates around Emergency Powers, the Crown Lands Bill, the Agriculture (Misc War Provisions) Act 1940 and the Beveridge Report. On one occasion I took the copy from the chair where Mr Churchill had been sitting during the debate. I still have this leaflet and I got it personally signed by one of the Commons police officers on duty on that day.

There was one day in particular on which I feel very pleased to have been present. That was the day in 1945 when the very first Scottish Nationalist MP took up his seat in the House of Commons. His name was Dr Robert Macintyre and he joined the House of Commons after winning the Motherwell by-election on 13th April 1945. He took to the floor and from memory I think he led a debate on education in Highland and Islands schools. To be present on that historic day was something special.

CHAPTER 17

Generals and Heroes

O NCE I got used to the work in Code and Cipher I really enjoyed it, although a lot of it became quite routine. We had all signed the Official Secrets Act and would never dream of discussing our work outside the office. We also had scrambler telephones in the office for added security. Even after the war, I never talked much about the work, knowing that we were only very minute cogs in a gigantic war machine. I never told my friends that the work was all done on machines, as I thought that would be a breach of security and I was amazed some years ago to read R.F. Jones's *Most Secret War* with detailed information about the workings of our cipher machines. Although we operated the machines, which were rather like old fashioned teleprinters (and were probably the forerunners of the modern computers), we had no idea how they worked and we had to call in the Royal and Mechanical Engineers when anything went wrong. Although I think the government was wrong in the way they handled the Peter Wright 'Spycatcher' affair, I think he was wrong, in many ways to breach the terms of the Official Secrets Act. I believe he could have conveyed all the facts he wished to convey without giving so much detail which resulted from his frustration about his treatment by the government.

We had our heroes during the war and one of mine, believe it or not, was the German General Erwin Rommel, whom General Montgomery called, "My Friendly Enemy". I could not think of him as a Nazi and just thought he was a very good soldier, doing the best he could for his country in the most humane way he could. I was horrified one day to receive a message which, once I had deciphered it, conveyed the news to Mr Churchill that Rommel had been forced to commit suicide after his part in a plot to assassinate Hitler had been uncovered. It was said that Hitler had given him the option of committing suicide or being strung up on piano wire, like some of the others involved in the plot. It feels strange to think that I had received and deciphered the message about Rommel before Mr Churchill could read it.

Of course, we didn't want Rommel to win any battles against us but we admired his strategy. Field Marshall Montgomery was worshipped by the troops. I noticed, from messages passing through my hands, that General Alexander (later 'of Tunis') was Monty's superior in the Mediterranean Command and was responsible for a lot of the strategy. Alexander didn't seem to have the same charisma as Monty and I don't expect he moved among the troops in the same way as Monty did, breaking a lot of rules about the wearing of uniform, just like myself but at a much higher level!

There was one general who was in constant touch with us, usually from different parts of the world. I think the last message from him that I deciphered was from our Military Mission in Chungking, China, towards the end of the war. His name fascinated me and I never forgot it. It was General Carton de Wiart and perhaps I remembered it as it faintly resembled Charles Dickens' Sidney Carton in *The Tale of Two Cities*. I never found out anything about this general through the messages I handled from him. However some years later after the war, I read a book by Freddie Spencer Chapman, whom I had met casually through my job with the National Fitness Council during the summer schools we ran at Guisachan and Gordon Castle. In this book General Carton de Wiart was mentioned and looking at the bibliography, I discovered that his biography had been published. I took a note of this and through my local lending library I was able to get the book which was lodged in the National Library of Scotland. The biography only covered the period between the two World Wars, when he owned an estate in Poland. Since reading the book I have seen the general's name mentioned in other books, one of which stated that, 'General Adrian Carton de Wiart won the Victoria Cross twice and lost an eye and a hand in World War I, while leading his men over the top in the Battle of the Somme, armed with a walking-stick and a pack of hand-grenades, pulling the pins out with his teeth.' In World War II one of his commands was the the Trondheim Fjord Expedition in Norway. Truly Carton de Wiart was a real hero, to my mind, and also a master of intelligence gathering. He certainly was not like one of Siegfried Sassoon's generals; indeed films and books have made heroes of much lesser men!

As the war went on and it was apparent that the Germans were going to be defeated, we hadn't so much urgent work. We were asked if we wanted a break to attend what was called a 'School of Military Intelligence'. I volunteered to go for three weeks to this school and made new friends there, encountering an old friend from my childhood days. This was an Inverness lad whose parents had also come from Lewis and whom we often visited. I hadn't seen him for years but we soon made up for lost time. I didn't learn much at this school, except how to do 'low-grade cipher', which was used in command posts. The colonel in charge of the school was rather a formidable character who tried to instill discipline and a great respect for the Official Secrets Act, telling us that, "It's not what you do. It's the way that you do it." We sang this over to ourselves, as those were the words of a current popular song of the day. He said, "That's the big secret which you must never tell, even after the war and even on your deathbed. You will be watched until you die." This colonel went round with a revolver in a holster, the only armed uniformed man I had ever seen. The policemen who looked at our passes when we were going in and out of War Office were the only people I saw with revolvers in their holsters. One of the friends I made at the school was a Scottish girl whose husband was stationed with the RAF near my husband in Belgium and they knew each other.

I don't think any of us at C6 would have been able to give much information to an enemy agent in any case, as we dealt with messages as and when they came in, according to priority. While one might have a message about a certain subject on a shift, perhaps there were no more messages on the same subject passing through the same hands. The priority ratings for the messages were 'Important', 'Most Important', 'Immediate', 'Most Immediate' and 'Emergency'. Once the Yanks came into the war, the Americanisations started and we had 'Top Secret' which was really a superfluous term, as they were all 'secret'. When on night duty I liked nothing better than to be singled out to do 'duds'. Those were messages that could not be enciphered owing to some corruption in the key to the cipher. One could spend a whole night trying to decipher one such message without success. The idea was never to give up if possible because if the message had to be repeated, there was more chance of the enemy cryptographers breaking the code. Sometimes the corruption would be because of a wrong letter picked up by the signallers who had received the message over the air. We had cards above our machines with all the letters of the alphabet in Morse code. In spite of this, all I remember of the Morse code are the two sequences which were more often transposed, namely, 'B' for 'V' and 'A' for 'N'. Sometimes, it would be some other mistake in the message and then we would have to go through a most laborious process called, the 'Thirty-nine Steps' because we had to take thirty-nine steps in the process. I sometimes wonder if John Buchan took the title for his famous book from this process, as he worked at the Foreign Office and would have been involved in cipher – or perhaps it was vice-versa. We had all sorts of words for describing parts of our work and 'rear-gunning' was one of them. The solving of a crossword always gives me a feeling of achievement but the solving of a 'dud' increased that feeling tenfold.

I recall one particular night duty when I was busy on 'duds'. This was the night of 5th/6th June, 1944, referred to now as 'D-Day'. Actually, we had received lots of messages referring to 'D-Day' as being 'Departure Day' for 'Overlord' which was the code-word for the invasion of Europe. No-one could predict accurately when the date would be because so much depended on weather and other circumstances. We were always on the alert for the great day and the idea of the 'Second Front' was on the lips of the general public, as well as the military. On that particular night I was allocated the job of working with 'duds' and settled down to try to solve a pile of corrupted messages that defied decipherment.

I think it was about 6 am that a huge batch of messages came in from Signals, most of them marked 'Emergency' and they all had to be attended to first. I was oblivious to all this at the time, being in a world of my own, stuck in a corner with my 'duds'. Some time later I was conscious of a lot of whispering and hilarity from the far side of the room and didn't pay much attention, as this often went on and relieved some of the intense concentration we usually had to apply to our work. So I carried on regardless, having only one more 'dud' to decipher. As I had been working on it for around two-and-a-half hours, I wasn't very confident of success. My brain seemed clogged and I distinctly remember lifting my head in surprise because I thought I heard the wail of the bagpipes, but it was only the variation in the hum of the air-conditioning.

At last, just before the day shift came on at 9 am, I managed to crack the last 'dud' and felt a great surge of relief, until my friend Joan D. came up and said, "Isn't it great news, Chris?" Feeling rather whacked and not really interested as I thought it was just news of another engagement, I said, "What news?" When she said, 'Overlord' I couldn't believe it! She added, "Don't tell me you didn't hear all the noise we made during the night?" I was stunned; there was I, thinking I had done so well by struggling with a message which contained only details about a cargo of ghee coming from the Far East, while all around me, history was being made! Talk about fiddling while Rome was burning! Ghee is a kind of buttery grease that had been used for greasing guns since the Indian Mutiny, which was supposed to have started after the charge that the British were using pig's fat or something similar which was taboo to the Indians. I have an autograph booked signed by all my War Office colleagues on that historic day back in June 1945.

I remember wondering sadly what had happened to my French teacher in Inverness Royal Academy, who had been engaged to a German professor pre-war. Had she married him and gone to live in Germany? Would she ever know that the first couplet from that lovely poem she had taught us by Paul Verlaine, 'Chanson d'Automne', had been used to alert the French Resistance leaders about the D-Day landings? This was one of my favourite French poems:

Les sanglots longs
Des violons
De l'autumne

Blessent mon cœur
D'une langueur
Monotone.

The long sobs
Of the violins
Of autumn

Wound my heart
With a monotonous
Languor.

I don't know who decided to use this poem; it seems a peculiar choice to incite an uprising, but perhaps that was why it was chosen.

When I heard later that Lord Lovat and his piper had been first to land on the beaches, I told myself that what I had heard during the long night had not been the hum of the air-conditioning but the echo from the ancient Highlanders' rallying call to battle, the pipes of war!

Don had at that time been posted back to Chichester from Ireland and he had arranged that I would go down there for my next 72-hours leave, instead of going to my brother's in Stowemarket. That arrangement was all cancelled when I got back to the house to find a manilla postcard addressed to me in Don's writing. On the other side there was no writing but a printed list of instructions and information with a tick against the one saying that Don had been posted overseas and that he would write me as soon as possible. That was the only time in the war that I remember being reduced to tears, usually being the one to comfort others in trouble. I went upstairs, sat on my bed and just howled. We hadn't met for over a year and it seemed particularly unfair. Then I had a brainwave because I had just noticed that the postcard was postmarked Winchester. I had a hurried breakfast, took the train to Winchester and tried to find out if any RAF personnel were still stationed there, as I knew he would have left Chichester. It was not the done thing to ask about the whereabouts of Army, Navy or Air Force personnel during the war and I soon gave up as I didn't see anyone in the uniform of the RAF. I then decided to do a bit of sight-seeing and went to Winchester Cathedral. When I was in the cathedral, I came across a stained-glass window dedicated to Isaak Walton, of *The Compleat Angler* fame. He was depicted sitting by a river bank with his fishing gear beside him and the words on the window were 'Study to be Quiet' from 1 Thessalonians. I felt that this fellow-fisherman somehow sympathised with me because Don and I had spent most of our summer holidays hunting the fish. Somehow or other I felt more relaxed and made a prayer in the cathedral that God would protect Don and send him safely home to me.

When word eventually came from Don it was to say that he had been posted to a Polish Squadron of the RAF. His companions had not a word of English and he had no knowledge of Polish. However he soon was able to pick it up and grew to admire the courage of the Polish and their ability to forage for the most unlikely foods and comforts, including perfume and silk stockings which were so scarce during the war. Don gave me some of this perfume, in a beautiful crystal bottle with a large stopper. This was so precious to me that I brought it home to Inverness and put it in a drawer in my bedroom. When I went to use it about a year afterwards, I found it had all evaporated! As for the silk stockings, I discovered one leg was longer than the other, although they wore well otherwise!

I don't know how they found each other but my brother Ian, who had been transferred from the 51st Highland to the 52nd Lowland Division, was now in the Royal Engineers and he was able to contact Don at Caen in France. They had a night out together just before the carnage there. Don told me later that it was awful, with railway lines twisted high up in the sky, buildings in rubble and piles of dead bodies heaped high, along with a terrible stench. Don went through the rest of the war with the Poles until finally they reached a camp very near to

Belsen, which was another horrific sight. While in that particular camp, which had just been evacuated by the Germans, he was astonished to see a map of the Island of Lewis (his native island) with a red flag stuck in one of the sea lochs there. He then remembered how one early morning in August 1939, when we were coming back in his brother's car from a night out, we had thought we noticed a small aeroplane with a black cross like the German markings flying over Gravir Loch and right across the island in the direction of the loch marked on the map. At the time we thought it strange, as war hadn't broken out at that time and we wondered why a German plane would be flying so low over our loch. However being young and carefree, it didn't really bother us at the time. When we went on leave to Lewis there had always been talk of suspected refuelling of German submarines in the sea lochs around Lewis and also of German so-called 'students' who had been holidaying in the island in the summer of 1939.

CHAPTER 18

Prince Monolulu's Racing Tips

MEANTIME, the Doodlebugs continued falling almost non-stop and we anxiously followed the progress of the Allied Forces with bated breath. However life went on in London in the same way, as we listened to Churchill's uplifting speeches, such as, "We shall fight on the beaches ..." By this time I noticed some of my friends debating about the kind of government we would have after the war. I was surprised at the way several of them spoke in support of Russia and a Socialist state. In its ideal state, I suppose communism sounded perfect; the same wages and conditions for everyone, no matter what kind of work they did, but I told myself that there would always be someone who didn't want to work and others who would bribe and cheat all the way. I suppose that, in a way, communism was similar to the old clan system, where the land was worked communally in the run-rig system where they rotated the crops and where the clan chief was regarded as a patriarchal figure. With the coming of the Union with England most clan chiefs usurped their patriarchal status and became lairds like English lords. They treated their clan lands and their clansmen as their own personal property to be cleared off and sent away to the Americas at their whim, although the land was originally only given to him for behoof of his clan and not as a personal possession.

Hearing all the talk about the marvellous things that were to happen 'when the boys came home', I wasn't surprised when in 1945 the Labour Party was swept into power as a result, it was said, of the soldiers' vote.

Being a person of fairly moderate views, except where the welfare of Scotland was concerned, my vote went to the Scottish National Party. I always considered it to be a classless party of all shades of opinion and status and I thought that once independence was won, then we would all vote on the issues of conservatism, socialism or liberalism of that day. I had listened to many speeches in the House of Commons and one of my worries was how we were to prevent Scotland from becoming a colony rather than a partner. However I sometimes wondered if Highlanders would be just as badly off under a Lowland central belt parliament as under Westminster.

We would often go to Hyde Park Speakers' Corner on a Sunday to hear the political harangues but I was more interested in 'Prince Monolulu' giving his racing tips. It wasn't that I was a punter (the only bet I ever made was back in Inverness when offices and housewives put a sixpenny bet on a horse through the office pool at the time of the Derby). I didn't understand what all the 'Prince's' antics were about but his outfit was colourful and he kept leaping about. The Prince wasn't Native American, but he dressed up as a chief, with a huge eagle feather headdress and he kept jumping and throwing his arms about as he shouted, "I gotta horse, I gotta horse." I believe he was English, although he wanted people to think he was a full blooded Native American. I remember once, when there was a British merchant seaman on a soap-box retelling the horrors of the Murmansk convoys and how we should all support Russia in her fight with the Germans, Monolulu kept shouting him down until I thought the two were going to come to blows; so we moved off in a hurry.

My friend Joan D. had fallen in love with and became engaged to an American captain she had met before she joined us at War Office. As her fiancé had also gone overseas, we consoled each other and tried not to worry about the danger our men faced. Joan belonged to Colchester, so we often travelled down together on the train as I took the same train to Stowemarket to visit my brother. In 1945 Joan married her Captain, Charles T Horner Jr, of the US Army. He later served as Major General and was highly decorated for outstanding leadership and extreme valour as Battalion Commander at Omaha Beach during the Normandy Landings, leading the First Infantry Division known as 'The Big Red One'. Many decorations followed during later military actions in North Africa and other theatres of war. After the war Joan and Charles did a lot of travelling when he was posted to France and they even did a tour of duty at Berchtesgaden, Hitler's 'Eagle's Nest' in Bavaria. They also visited Okinawa and then to the Pentagon in Washington where they settled. She and I always kept in touch, usually just cards and long letters at Christmas. Joan and her husband visited me in Skye some years ago and, although I had an open invitation to visit them in Washington, I never did so. After the war, Joan had a family of five; four sons (two now in the Army) and one daughter and my family consisted of four daughters and one son. We had a lot of common interests in our families. Joan used to say to me that if I didn't keep in touch with her after I was demobbed, she wouldn't send me nylon stockings from America, but she did send them. Before long they were also easily available in Britain.

CHAPTER 19

The Long Journey Home

ONCE it was clear that we were going to win the war, we all looked forward to shedding that awful khaki uniform, settling down to make a home with our husbands and starting a family. The rule for demobilisation was first in, first out and, being one of the original peacetime volunteers, I was one of the first to be demobbed. Thinking of the journey home reminded me of the poem by A M Harbord:

At Euston (by one who is not going)

Stranger with the pile of luggage
Proudly labelled for Portree,
How I wish this night of August
I were you and you were me!
Think of all that lies before you
When the train goes sliding forth.
And the lines athwart the sunset
Lead you swiftly to the North!
Think of breakfast at Kingussie,
Think of high Drumochter Pass.
Think of Highland breezes singing
Through the bracken and the grass.
Scabious blue and yellow daisy,
Tender fern beside the train,

Rowdy Tummel falling, brawling,
Seen and lost and glimpsed again!
You will pass my golden roadway
Of the days of long ago:
Will you realise the magic
Of the names I used to know;
Clachnaharry, Achnashellach,
Achnasheen and Duirinish?
Ev'ry moor alive with coveys,
Every pool aboil with fish;
Every well-remembered vista
More exciting by the mile
Till the wheeling gulls are screaming
Round the engine at the Kyle
Think of cloud on Bheinn na Cailleach,
Jagged Cuillins soaring high
Scent of peat and all the glamour
Of the misty Isle of Skye!
Rods and gun case in the carriage,
Wise retriever in the van;
Go, and good luck travel with you!
(Wish I'd half your luck, my man!)

I was lucky enough to meet my army friend Flora (First Aid Nursing Yeomanry) from Inverness on the same train. In true British muddling fashion, the train left London and then went in the wrong direction and we all had to get out and join a different train. At first the train was very quiet but as soon as we crossed over the border into Scotland, the train erupted into joyous music. I heard the sound of an accordion, then the bagpipes and soon the whole train was in uproar as everyone celebrated the end of the war. It was a truly wonderful journey home after being demobbed at Redford Barracks in Edinburgh. What marvellous plans we had for the future, although maybe some of them turned out like Robert Burns's lines, 'The best laid schemes o' mice and men gang aft agley' … but that's another story!

In spite of all the hardships, air-raids and deprivations, I would never regret joining the ATS and the camaraderie among my colleagues, members of the other Forces and amongst the civilian population was marvellous.

Before leaving War Office, I had been offered three options. I could stay on at War Office as a civilian, remaining in code and cipher, as the work would continue even in peacetime. The government also offered to put me through any university of my choice to study in whatever subjects I wished to further my career. I could also seek demobilisation from the ATS and return to civilian life with a gratuity from the government.

As I had married in 1943 and wanted to set up home with my husband and bring up children, my choice was the third option. I have never regretted making this choice. It led to my living in the islands and eventually holding down three jobs; one in charge of the Executry and Trust department of a legal firm, one as Registrar of Births, Marriages and Deaths and Census Officer for North Skye and the other as official Court Shorthand Writer in the Sheriff Courts in the islands and on occasions on the mainland. Looking back, I had achieved my early ambitions to live and work in the islands and fulfil my other ambitions of becoming a career-girl, wife and mother!

The years spent working in wartime London were intense and we lived each day not knowing whether we would survive or not, but looking back indeed, 'Bliss was it in that dawn to be alive. But to be young was very Heaven'.

I have told my children that when my days do reach an end, then they should remember Christina Rossetti's lines 'Better by far you should forget and smile, than you should remember and be sad.' But if anyone must shed a tear, then do so just once a year, in November when the poppies are for sale. Give generously then in memory of my generation's lost youth and the lost values we fought for.